THE
GRAND PRIX
RIDERS

THE
GRAND PRIX
RIDERS

MICK WOOLLETT & PETER CLIFFORD

HAZLETON PUBLISHING

1985

PUBLISHER
Richard Poulter

EXECUTIVE PUBLISHER
Elizabeth Le Breton

ART EDITOR
Steve Small

PRODUCTION MANAGER
George Greenfield

PRODUCTION CONTROLLER
Peter Lovering

PRODUCTION ASSISTANT
Deirdre Fenney

This first edition published in 1990
by Hazleton Publishing,
3 Richmond Hill, Richmond,
Surrey TW10 6RE.

ISBN: 0-905138-66-X

Printed in Spain by Graficas Estella
SA, Estella

Typeset by First Impression
Graphics Ltd, Richmond, Surrey

Colour reproduction by Adroit
Photo Litho Ltd, Birmingham

DISTRIBUTORS

UK & Other Markets

Osprey Publishing Ltd
59 Grosvenor Street
London W1X 9DA

NORTH AMERICA
Motorbooks International
PO Box 2
729 Prospect Avenue
Osceola
Wisconsin 54020, USA

Paul Oxman Publishing
17165 Newhope
Unit M
Fountain Valley
CA 92708, USA

AUSTRALIA
Technical Book & Magazine Co. Pty
289-299 Swanston Street
Melbourne
Victoria 3000

Universal Motor Publications
c/o Automoto Motoring Bookshop
152-154 Clarence Street
Sydney 2000
New South Wales

NEW ZEALAND
David Bateman Ltd
PO Box 65062
Mairangi Bay
Auckland 10

Title page: **Flat out. Kenny Roberts (Yamaha) leads Freddie Spencer (Honda) during the 500 cc class of the 1983 Dutch TT. Kenny won this race but Freddie took the title.**

Left: **Looking ahead. Barry Sheene (Suzuki) heads for third place in the 500 cc class of the South African Grand Prix at Kyalami in 1983. It proved to be the last time that he finished among the top three in a World Championship race.**

INTRODUCTION

THE odd thing about this book is that it has not been done before – in any language! A great deal has been written about motor cycle road racing and about the machines and personalities that have graced the sport since the World Championships were introduced in 1949 – but as far as I know not one of them is remotely similar to this one.

In this book you will find a picture of every World Champion and one of virtually every rider who scored a 'near miss' – many of the latter being more famous than the lesser title winners.

With every picture there is a pen-portrait in which Peter Clifford and I have attempted to bring out the character of the rider as well as list his major achievements.

My own career in racing, first as spectator, then as helper/mechanic, sidecar passenger, reporter and finally photographer, spans the years from 1949 to the early Eighties so I had the good fortune to know the great majority of the people I have written about.

In fact, many long-forgotten moments were rekindled for me as I searched through my bits and pieces – memories of wonderful days and great characters, many of whom sadly died racing motor cycles.

Peter is just as familiar with the 1980s – a decade when the sport has flourished into a new 'golden age' thanks to the enthusiasm of Japanese industry and the major sponsors.

Where possible the pictures used were taken at the time of the rider's greatest achievements, and I must thank Nick Nicholls for providing many of the outstanding portrait shots. I also thank my continental colleagues, Maurice Bula of Switzerland, Carlo Perelli of Italy, Helmut Krackowizer of Austria and Karl Schleuter of Germany, for answering my plea for photographs we did not have.

To get you talking, and arguing, there is a section in which four of us give our selection of the top ten Grand Prix riders of the World Championship era – not an easy task! To augment the views of Peter Clifford and myself we enlisted the aid of Denis Jenkinson, sidecar passenger with Eric Oliver in 1949 who, despite his worldwide fame as a motor racing journalist, has always kept a keen eye on our sport, and John Brown, who reported the big races for many years for *Motor Cycle News*.

A final word of thanks – this time to all Grand Prix competitors. I am all too aware that we have had to leave out many fine riders and give others only the briefest of mentions. Having said that, I am sure that this book will be a worthwhile addition to your library and one which you'll be able to delve into from time to time to settle arguments and refresh your memory.

Mick Woollett
Hemel Hempstead
January 1990

THE FIFTIES

Umberto Masetti (Gilera) leads Geoff Duke (Norton) during the 1952 Dutch TT. The four-cylinder Italian machine was far faster than the Norton and the Italian won the race – and the championship.

By MICK WOOLLETT

Crunch! The suspension of Geoff Duke's four-cylinder Gilera bottoms out as he lands after jumping Ballaugh Bridge *(left)* during his winning ride in the 1955 Senior TT.

F ROM the word go Geoff Duke was a sensation. Wearing tight-fitting one-piece leathers he looked as if he came from a different planet from his rivals in their baggy, padded two-piece suits. And once the race started the difference was even more clear-cut.

Taking advantage of the superb road-holding capacity of the brand new Featherbed Nortons that, by happy coincidence, made their début when Duke was promoted into the team for the 1950 season, he swept into corners faster and laid his machine over further than anyone had before. Geoff's style was perfection. Knees and elbows tucked in, chin on the tank, he made it look so effortless that those of us who were lucky enough to see him in action on the Nortons still talk about it with awe.

By today's standards Duke came late to road racing. Born in St Helens, Lancashire in 1923 he learned his motor cycling as a despatch rider in the Royal Signals. After the war he took up trials riding and scrambling and was good enough to catch Norton's eye. He was offered a weekday job at the factory, with machines to ride in off-road events at the weekends.

Far left: Geoff Duke in action in 1951 – the year he became the first double World Champion, winning both 350 cc and 500 cc titles on works Nortons.

However, his real ambition was to go road racing and he was soon winning, first the 1949 Senior Clubman's TT for sports machines on a Norton International, then the Senior Manx Grand Prix on a 'Garden-gate' Norton in the September of that year.

Duke's talent was undeniable and for 1950 he moved on to the international scene – and kept on winning, first at the Senior TT, then on the continent. But faulty tyres put him out of the Dutch and Belgian rounds and, despite winning the final event in Italy, he lost the 500 cc title by a single point.

He completely dominated in 1951, though, winning both the 350 cc and 500 cc World Championships and establishing himself with the British public to such an extent that he was voted 'Sportsman of the Year' by the readers of a national daily.

Behind the scenes all was not well. He was still treated as a relatively poorly paid 'hired hand' by Norton, and he could see that unless the factory developed new machines they would soon be outpaced by the multi-cylinder Italian opposition. A crash in 1952 brought things to a head and Norton enthusiasts were stunned when he joined the Italian Gilera team for 1953.

Duke won the 500 cc crown three years running for Gilera – then came problems. First there was a scandalous six-month suspension for siding with lesser lights at the Dutch TT, then a crash early in 1957, and finally the decision by Gilera to quit racing at the end of 1957.

Geoff battled on, riding a variety of machines and scoring occasional wins. But the old magic had gone and most were relieved when he announced his retirement in May 1960.

An incredibly youthful looking old age pensioner, he now lives in the Isle of Man, scene of so many of his triumphs.

World Champion: 500 cc 1951, 1953, 1954 & 1955.   350 cc 1951 & 1952

FITNESS paid off for Freddie Frith. A teetotaller, non-smoker and jogger long before such things became fashionable, his career was one of the few that spanned the war and culminated in him winning the 350 cc World Championship at the age of 40.

A Lincolnshire man, Freddie hit the motor cycling headlines when he rode a Velocette into third place in the very first Manx Grand Prix back in 1930. At that time the Manx (popularly known as the Amateur TT) was the nursery ground for British factory teams and, after winning the 500 cc race on a Norton in 1935, Frith joined the Birmingham factory for the 1936 season.

He was an immediate success, winning the 1936 Junior TT and the 1937 Senior (during which he clocked the first-ever lap around the Isle of Man at over 90 mph). In fact, in the eight TTs in which he rode for Norton he only once finished outside the first three and that was in 1939 when he retired from the Junior with machine trouble.

He spent the war years as a motor cycle instructor in the army and although, in his own opinion, he was not riding as well as he had in the Thirties, he was still good enough to win all the five Grands Prix that constituted the 350 cc World Championship in 1949 – now Velocette mounted.

Modest, quietly spoken, typically British, Freddie retired to run a motor cycle business in Grimsby, where he died in 1988.

A N also-ran before 1939, Les Graham served as a bomber pilot during the war and, after joining the Plumstead-based AJS team, became one of the first stars of the Forties.

His mounts were the then-new single-cylinder 350 cc 7R and the very different 500 cc twin – known as the Porcupine, because of the spiky finning on the cylinder head which jutted forward between the downtubes of the frame.

Born in Wallasey on the Wirral peninsula in 1911, Les was outpaced by the faster Velocettes in the 350 cc class of those early World Championship races. In the bigger class, though, he fought and won an epic battle with the strong Gilera team to take the 1949 500 cc title by a single point.

Unfortunately for Les the Porcupine failed to live up to its early promise and after a series of frustrating problems, including a magneto drive failure that robbed him of victory just miles from the end of the 1949 Senior TT, he left AJS.

After a year freelancing he was signed by MV Agusta. He responded by taking second place in the 1952 500 cc series with wins in the Italian and Spanish rounds.

He achieved the TT win that had eluded him for so long when he won the 125 cc race in 1953. A day later he was dead. His ill-handling 500 cc four-cylinder MV Agusta went out of control at 120 mph on Bray Hill and the motor cycle world was stunned by the loss of this smiling sportsman.

BRUNO RUFFO

NELLO PAGANI

SERVED in the Italian contingent on the Russian front in the war. Won three championships, the 250 cc for Moto Guzzi in 1949 and 1951 and, Mondial mounted, the 125 cc in 1950.

THE aristocratic Italian who won the first 125 cc championship for Mondial and who finished second on a Gilera in the 500 cc class. Later managed the MV Agusta team.

World Champion: 250 cc 1949 & 1951

World Champion: 125 cc 1950

World Champion: 125 cc 1949

ENRICO LORENZETTI

LIBERO LIBERATI

TALL and thin, he scored all his successes on Moto Guzzi machines, including winning the 250 cc title in 1952 at the age of 41.

FAIR haired and stockily built, Liberati took over from Geoff Duke to win the 500 cc title for Gilera in 1957. Lost his life in a road accident in 1962.

World Champion: 250 cc 1952

World Champion: 500 cc 1957

A classic shot that captures the thrill of those early sidecar races – Eric Oliver and Lorenzo Dobelli (Norton–Watsonian) head for victory in the 1952 Spanish Grand Prix.

World Champion: Sidecars 1949, 1950, 1951 & 1953

QUITE simply, Eric Oliver was the supreme sidecar racer of his era – and probably of all time. He combined technical skill, riding ability and self-confidence with a truly awesome will to win that often had the opposition beaten before the race began.

Like the Americans who currently dominate the 500 cc solo class he learned his trade on the dirt – on the grass tracks of England. Spinning wheels and a sliding outfit, usually with the front wheel pointing anywhere but the direction of travel, held no terror for Eric.

Born in Crowborough in the Sussex countryside in 1911 Oliver was an accomplished solo racer, finishing eighth and tenth on Velocettes in the 1948 Junior and Senior TTs before devoting his talents almost entirely to the three-wheelers.

With Denis Jenkinson in the chair he dominated the 1949 World Championship on his Norton–Watsonian outfit – powered that year by a 600 cc single-cylinder Manx engine. For 1950 the limit was reduced to 500 cc and many felt that Oliver would struggle against the far faster four-cylinder Gilera of Italian Ercole Frigerio.

To Eric it was a challenge. With Lorenzo Dobelli of Italy replacing Jenks he continued to dominate. There were a couple of hiccups caused by accidents, notably in 1952 when a crash in a non-championship race in France cost Oliver his chance that year, and in 1954 when a prang while competing in a hill-climb in Germany put him out of contention.

Despite these setbacks he remained the man to beat. He won the Belgian Grand Prix for six years in succession, partnered by five different passengers: Jenks, Dobelli, Stanley Price (a one-race stand-in), Stan Dibben and Les Nutt.

It was at the Belgian event in 1954 that Oliver set a trend – he appeared on a fully streamlined machine with kneeler riding position – a lead eventually followed by all sidecar competitors. The previous year he had won using a conventional Norton–Watsonian outfit without any streamlining, averaging 90.55 mph.

Late in 1953 Eric assisted Norton as second rider to solo star Ray Amm in a series of successful record attempts at the Montlhéry track near Paris. After Amm had broken numerous short-distance figures they shared the riding for the longer ones (including the 1000 kilometres at 119 mph). The machine was Norton's Flying Fish, very low built, with the rider stretching forward from a kneeling position.

With the help of Watsonian, the Birmingham sidecar makers, Oliver built that kneeler outfit for 1954 and pushed his winning speed for the Belgian up to 94.2 mph. But age and the increasing speed of the works BMWs finally persuaded Eric to retire in 1955, although he remained a formidable rival in vintage races well into his 60s.

BORN in 1926, in Parma, Umberto Masetti was brought up amid motor cycles for his father was the local Gilera agent. He started racing in 1946 and, riding a Moto Morini, won the 125 cc Italian championship in 1949.

His potential was spotted by Gilera team-manager Piero Taruffi, the former motor cycle and car racer and record breaker, who signed him for the 1950 season. He was soon locked in combat with Geoff Duke, who was blazing a trail on the new Featherbed Norton. Truth to tell, in those early days, Masetti was no match for Duke. The sudden transition from lightweight to 140 mph fire-engine was just too much, and was not helped by the fact that the Gilera, though fast, did not handle anything like so well as the Norton.

Nevertheless, the dashing young Italian with the dark and flashing good looks of a film star persevered and when the entire Norton team were forced to pull out of both the Dutch TT and Belgian GP with tyre troubles he calmly took over to win.

Switching from Dunlop to Avon, Duke and the Norton were fast enough to win at the quickest circuit used that year – Monza, for the Italian Grand Prix. There, within earshot of the Gilera factory at Arcore, Duke won at 102.39 mph but Masetti was second – which was enough to give him the 500 cc title by a single point.

Masetti, with Mickey Mouse on the front of his helmet, slumped to third in the title chase the following year. But he came back strongly to outpace Duke fair and square in both the Dutch and Belgian in 1952 and regained the title. His reward was to be replaced by Duke in the Gilera team for 1953. Disgusted, he left to join MV Agusta but was never again to figure in the championship chase.

INCREDIBLY the racing career of Fergus Anderson spanned almost 30 years, from when he started in local events in 1927 until he lost his life in a racing accident in Belgium in 1956.

In pre-war days Fergus, who liked nothing better than a round of golf, was one of the earliest members of the 'continental circus': they used to travel around Europe by car and train, competing where and when they could. In those days he rode Velocettes, Nortons and a 350 cc NSU which, though not as fast as the British machines, would earn him more starting money in Germany – Fergus was always a good businessman!

It was only after the war, which he spent in the merchant navy, that Fergus (born and bred in Surrey, despite the very Scottish name) blossomed into a top-flight rider.

A cosmopolitan character, he managed to catch the eye of Moto Guzzi. During a near ten-year association with the Italian company he raced successfully in 250, 350 and 500 cc events, winning a total of 12 Grands Prix and two 350 cc World Championships.

Unfortunately he then had a disagreement with Moto Guzzi, left them, and returned to the ranks of the continental circus to race a 500 cc BMW. It proved a fatal move for, at the age of 47, he crashed at Floreffe and was killed minutes after setting a new lap record.

Light and low. Fergus Anderson on the Moto Guzzi with which he won the 350 cc title in 1954.

World Champion: 350 cc 1953 & 1954

Team-work. Willi Noll and passenger Fritz Cron in action in the 1954 Swiss Grand Prix on their partially streamlined BMW outfit.

WITH massive assistance from BMW it was little Willi Noll who finally got the better of the British Norton duo of Oliver and Smith to win the Sidecar World Championship for Germany in 1954.

It had been a long, hard struggle which started when West Germany was readmitted to the international scene for the 1952 season. By 1954 BMW were using fuel injection and Noll's factory machine had far better acceleration than the Nortons – though the British single still had the edge on top speed.

Eric Oliver won the first three Grands Prix that year and looked set to take his fifth title, but an accident in a minor event effectively ended his season. And it was Noll, with passenger Fritz Cron, who came good to win the final three rounds and take the crown. Later in 1954 Noll upped the one-hour sidecar record to 106.39 mph and the standing start 10 kilometre to 132.6 mph.

A scholarly figure with round face and glasses, Noll made a disastrous start in 1955 when he failed to finish in the first two races. He was then beaten in both the German and Dutch rounds by compatriot Willi Faust. Noll turned the tables to beat Faust after a fantastic dice in the Belgian Grand Prix – by one second!

That second place clinched the title for Faust but when he was seriously injured early in 1956 Noll took over to win his second World Championship. He and passenger Cron retired at the end of the season and in 1957 Noll tried his hand at car racing.

In recent years he has served the sport as an official and was recently elected a vice-president of the sport's governing body, the Fédération Internationale Motocycliste.

CYRIL SMITH

TUBBY, balding and bespectacled, Cyril Smith was not the film-maker's idea of a motor cycle racer. Yet when Eric Oliver was sidelined by injury in 1952, it was Cyril who took over to win the sidecar title for Norton and for England.

A part-time racer in previous years, Cyril had quit his job at Norton to go full-time racing, but the season started disastrously when he crashed during practice for a minor international race at Mettet in Belgium and suffered head injuries. The doctor told him he would never compete again – yet three weeks later he rode a brilliant race at the Swiss Grand Prix in Berne to finish second, just five seconds behind Albino Milani on the far faster four-cylinder Gilera.

After a series of tremendous races, notably the German Grand Prix at Solitude near Stuttgart where he pulled out of the slipstream of Ernesto Merlo's Gilera to win by a few yards, Cyril and passenger Bob Clements clinched the title.

Unfortunately it was all downhill after that for the former Tank Corps sergeant-major from Birmingham. Although he continued to be a top class sidecar racer he refused to switch from his beloved Norton engines to the faster BMWs, and he gradually slipped out of the reckoning.

In June 1959 he finally quit at the age of 40 to start a new career as a service manager. Things did not work out and he committed suicide – a sad end for a likeable man who had given pleasure to thousands, and to whom I owe a personal debt, for it was as passenger with Cyril in 1956 that I started my own racing career.

Cyril Smith and passenger Bob Clements head for second place in the 1952 Swiss Grand Prix on their Norton–Watsonian, a vital result in their championship-winning year.

I N the first decade of World Championship road racing Cecil Sandford was the only British rider to win a title in the lightweight classes – and the fact that he took both the 125 cc and 250 cc crowns in different years and on different makes shows just how sought after his talents were.

Lean and wiry, Cecil was born in Gloucestershire in 1928, and he looked every inch a racer. He learned his trade racing Velocettes, with sponsorship from Arthur Taylor, a dealer in Shipston-on-Stour whose daughter Pat he later married.

He got his break in 1952 when Les Graham recommended him to MV Agusta for a works ride in the 125 cc TT. Cecil won the race easily, beating Carlo Ubbiali on the rival Mondial. MV Agusta kept him on their bikes for that season and he responded by winning the World Championship for them.

In 1953 the MV Agustas were outpaced by the new NSUs but Sandford still managed second place in the championship. A spell on Moto Guzzis and the three-cylinder two-stroke 350 cc DKW followed, with Cecil taking fourth place in the World Championship in 1956 on the German machine before he joined Mondial for the 1957 season.

That year the beautifully engineered, fully streamlined Mondials completely dominated the quarter-litre class, with Sandford winning the title from team-mates Tarquinio Provini and future trials supremo Sammy Miller. But at the end of the season Mondial pulled out of racing and so did Cecil.

Now retired from the motor business he took over from his father-in-law, Cecil spends much of his time restoring antique furniture.

World Champion: 250 cc 1957.   125 cc 1952

WERNER HAAS

SHORT and dark, little Werner Haas looked more like an Italian than a German – and he acted like one, too, with his ready smile and outgoing personality.

Born in Augsburg in 1927 he began motor cycling in 1947 on an old NSU and his rise to racing stardom was meteoric. He started the 1952 season, totally unknown, racing an Austrian Puch. But, as luck would have it, the German NSU factory were planning an onslaught on the Grands Prix and were developing new and very sophisticated four-stroke racers – a single-cylinder 125 cc and a twin 250 cc.

Starting from scratch they had no riders and decided to give the little Bavarian a try. He went straight out and won the 125 cc class of the German Grand Prix at Solitude, beating Carlo Ubbiali (Mondial) and Cecil Sandford (MV Agusta), the two top men of the day.

Proving it was no flash in the pan he went to the Italian Grand Prix at Monza and finished second in the 250 cc class. Encouraged, NSU built new machines for 1953 and Werner walked away with both 125 cc and 250 cc titles – the first German to win a motor cycle World Championship and only the second person to score a championship double (Geoff Duke was the first, in 1951).

Haas kept up the pace in 1954. He won five 250 cc Grands Prix in succession and averaged over 90 mph when he won the class in the Isle of Man, shattering both lap and race records by enormous margins.

When NSU pulled out of racing at the end of the year Haas retired, only to lose his life in a flying accident the following year.

Little Werner Haas on the beautifully engineered 250 cc NSU twin at Ballacraine during the 1953 Lightweight TT.

World Champion: 250 cc 1953 & 1954.   125 cc 1953

CARLO UBBIALI

COOL, calculating and seldom smiling, Carlo Ubbiali exhibited none of the fiery temperament and windmill hand-gestures favoured by the majority of his Italian colleagues – and his riding reflected his nature. Nothing seemed to upset the little man, who was born in Bergamo in 1929. He was completely unflappable and simply got on with the business of winning races, doing this so successfully that he ended up with a tally of nine World Championships and 39 Grand Prix wins – all achieved in the 125 cc and 250 cc classes.

Ubbiali began making news in 1949 when he proved he was a real all-rounder by finishing third on a Mondial in the first 125 cc World Championship and winning a gold medal in the gruelling International Six Days Trial, held that year in Wales.

The following year he won the Italian 125 cc championship for sports machines, for Mondial, and his first Grand Prix – the 125 cc class of the Ulster, in which only he and his Mondial team-mate Bruno Ruffo finished! For 1951 he stayed with Mondial and rode their beautifully built little double overhead camshaft four-stroke to his first World Championship.

Beaten by Cecil Sandford (MV Agusta) in 1952 Ubbiali switched to the rival Italian team for the following year, but the German NSU factory had the upper hand and it was not until 1955 that Ubbiali triumphed again. In 1956 he went one better by winning both the 125 cc and 250 cc World Championships for MV Agusta.

Five more World Championships followed before the death of his brother, Maurizio, coupled with MV Agusta's waning interest in racing, prompted his retirement at

Style of a lightweight champion: Carlo Ubbiali guns his 125 cc MV Agusta to victory in an international event in Madrid in 1959.

the end of the 1960 season. He left the sport as undisputed lightweight champion, having scored the double for MV Agusta in both 1959 and 1960 – a fact recognised by the Italian public, who voted him their 'Sportsman of the Year' for 1960. It was a fitting reward for a truly outstanding rider who, despite being at the top for so long, never had a serious accident.

World Champion: 250 cc 1956, 1959 & 1960.   125 cc 1951, 1955, 1956, 1958, 1959 & 1960

THE first Australian, in fact the first non-European, to win a road racing World Championship (two years before Jack Brabham took Formula One honours), Keith Campbell was a typical member of that happy-go-lucky gang of Commonwealth riders who did so much to liven up those early post-war years.

Born in Melbourne in 1931, Keith followed his elder brother George into racing and in 1951 set out for England with a 350 cc Velocette to ride in the Manx Grand Prix. He held third place until he lost his way in fog and crashed.

After a stay in hospital he sailed home and worked flat out to save enough money for a second shot at the amateur race in the Island. He had no luck but decided to stay in Europe that winter anyway and have a crack at the continent the next year. He got a job on the production line at the old Norton factory in Bracebridge Street, Birmingham, and in 1953 established himself with placings on the continent.

By 1955 he was the most successful non-works rider in Europe and his big, black mud-spattered American car with trailer containing three battered Nortons was a familiar sight from Finland to Spain.

For 1956 he joined Moto Guzzi, racing the lightweight 350 cc and fearsome 500 cc V8 – going on to win the 350 cc World Championship in 1957. But in September that year Moto Guzzi quit racing and Keith, who married Geoff Duke's sister-in-law Geraldine Reid the same month, decided to cash in on his title by having just one last season in Europe, racing his own Nortons.

It proved a fateful decision. Keith was killed when he skidded on oil at a minor international meeting at Cadours in France. Those who knew him will remember him as cheerful, resourceful and a good friend.

World Champion: 350 cc 1957

The combination of Tarquinio Provini and Mondial were hard to beat in 1957. Here the dashing Italian leads the 250 cc Italian Grand Prix at Monza. He won at an average speed of 109.44 mph.

N O man rode so hard for so long as Tarquinio Provini, a tough, swarthy Italian who seemed to be perpetually fighting as a lone underdog – particularly in his later years, when he battled alone against the growing might of the Japanese in the 250 cc class.

Riding for Mondial he worked his way up the ladder, winning the 125 cc Italian title in 1955, the 175 cc category the following year, and then the 125 cc World Championship in 1957. When Mondial quit at the end of that season Provini, born in 1933 in Piacenza, switched to MV Agusta.

There he made an uneasy team-mate for Carlo Ubbiali – two hard men, both determined to win, making things difficult for team-manager Nello Pagani. Provini won the 250 cc title for the Gallarate factory in 1958 but, after two years of playing second fiddle to Ubbiali, joined the little Morini factory for 1960.

At first there were setbacks, due to lack of finance and crashes, but gradually the single-cylinder four-stroke Morini, brilliantly ridden by Provini, became more and more of a threat to the Honda and Yamaha teams in the keenly contested 250 cc class. And in 1963 Provini failed by just two points to take the crown from Jim Redman and Honda. Incredibly the little Morini won the fastest 250 cc race that year, the German Grand Prix at Hockenheim, at an average speed of 116.26 mph.

Provini switched to racing the new 250 cc four-cylinder Benelli in 1964 and battled on with his distinctive flat-on-the-tank style, scoring the occasional win. A terrible high-speed crash in the Isle of Man in 1966 finally put him out of the sport for good, though happily he did eventually make a full recovery.

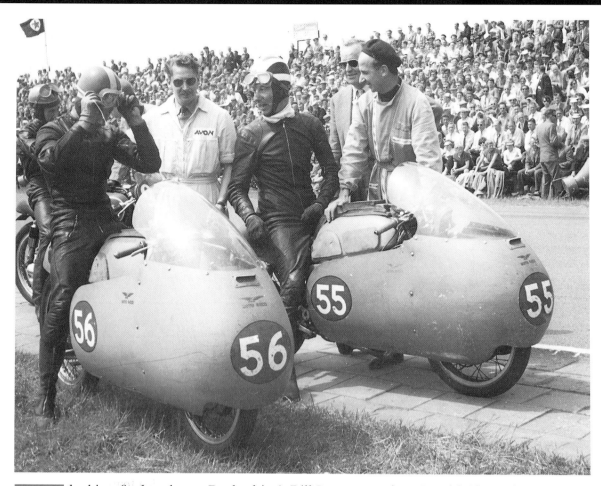

A leaking fuel tank cost Derbyshire's Bill Lomas a unique World Championship double in 1955, when he was so sought after that he was able to organise a contract with the MV Agusta factory for the 250 cc class and with rivals Moto Guzzi for the 350 cc division.

A clear-cut winner of the 350 cc crown on the fully streamlined and incredibly light Moto Guzzi, he lost the quarter-litre title when he was disqualified from first place in the Dutch TT because he failed to kill his engine during a brief precautionary pit stop to take on fuel.

Bill went on to win the 350 cc title for a second time in 1956, when he also raced the mighty eight-cylinder Moto Guzzi in 500 cc races. But a crash in a non-championship event at Imola early in 1957 followed by another accident in Holland and the withdrawal of Moto Guzzi at the end of the year cut short his career.

Son of a motor cycle dealer, Bill started racing at Cadwell Park in 1946 when he was still at school. In the early days he rode JAP- and Royal Enfield-powered specials. Technically talented, he converted a Royal Enfield engine from pushrod to double overhead camshaft valve operation and won many short circuit races with it.

He progressed to Velocette and then factory AJS machines before catching the eye of MV Agusta, NSU, and finally Moto Guzzi, with whom he scored his greatest successes. After retiring he continued in the motor cycle trade and still takes a lively interest in two-wheeled affairs, particularly classic racing events.

Speaking of his early retirement, Bill says: 'It was probably all for the best. The bikes were far too fast for the tyres. A lot who kept on aren't here now.'

DARIO AMBROSINI

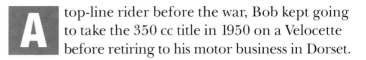

BOB FOSTER

THE first champion to be killed in a racing accident. He won the 250 cc title for Benelli in 1950 only to lose his life at the French Grand Prix at Albi the next year.

A top-line rider before the war, Bob kept going to take the 350 cc title in 1950 on a Velocette before retiring to his motor business in Dorset.

World Champion: 250 cc 1950

World Champion: 350 cc 1950

RUPERT HOLLAUS

WALTER SCHNEIDER

THE fourth of the German squad helped by BMW, Walter and passenger Hans Strauss *(below left)* outlasted and outlived their rivals to win the title in 1958 and 1959.

World Champion: Sidecars 1958 & 1959

WILLI FAUST

A gentle giant of a man, Willi won the 1955 sidecar title for BMW with passenger Karl Remmert *(above left)* but was so severely injured early the following year that he never raced again.

THE blond Austrian won the 125 cc crown for the German NSU factory in 1954 but was killed in an accident at Monza in September that year.

World Champion: 125 cc 1954

World Champion: Sidecars 1955

DURING the war Fritz had one of the most dangerous jobs going – he piloted planes full of petrol across the Mediterranean to keep Rommel's army on the move. With passenger Manfred Grunwald he won the 1957 sidecar title on a works BMW but was killed in an accident at Bilbao in August that year.

KNOWN as H-P, raced on two and four wheels before the war (including the rear-engined Auto Union) and won the 250 cc title on an NSU Sportmax in 1955 at the age of 46.

World Champion: Sidecars 1957

World Champion: 250 cc 1955

JOHN SURTEES

Left: **In 1957 the 500 cc MV Agusta was not fast enough to beat the Gileras. Here John Surtees guns the four-cylinder machine out of Governors Bridge during TT practice.**

COMBINING his natural talents of technical ability and riding skill with a single-minded ambition to succeed, John Surtees was *the* outstanding rider of the second half of the 1950s. He quit at the end of the 1960 season as undisputed top dog – going on to become the first and so far only man to win World Championships on both two and four wheels.

Father Jack was a big, burly motor cycle dealer from south London, a formidable competitor in the sidecar class at local grass track and road races, using mainly Norton-powered machines. And when he was old enough John became passenger – in ill-fitting helmet, baggy leathers and despatch rider's boots.

An engineering apprentice he was soon competing himself and first caught the eye when, aged 17, he raced a home-tuned Vincent Grey Flash at Thruxton in 1951 and twice finished second to the then-unbeatable combination of Geoff Duke and his factory Norton.

Learning his craft. John Surtees (Norton) at Scarborough in 1954.

Switching to Nortons for the 350 cc and 500 cc classes, and adding an NSU for the 250 cc, John became the dominant figure on British short circuits – in 1955 winning 65 out of a total of 72 races he entered!

Inevitably he moved into international racing, scoring his first success on a 250 cc NSU in the Ulster Grand Prix in 1955, and towards the end of the year he signed for MV Agusta. He immediately repaid the Italian factory by taking the 500 cc World Championship in 1956.

Quiet and shy, John was always a loner with something of a chip on his shoulder. Confident in his own ability he felt frustrated when others criticised him. He thought deeply about his racing and his mechanical ability stood him in good stead when it came to sorting out problems with the machines he was racing.

After a lean 1957 he took over as complete boss of the 350 cc and 500 cc classes when the rival Gilera and Moto Guzzi factories quit racing at the end of 1957. During the three-year spell from 1958 until he retired at the end of 1960 to go car racing, John won 33 of the 40 classic races held and was the first man ever to win the Senior class of the Isle of Man TT for three years in succession.

Now, after his years in car racing both as driver and constructor, John is back on the bike scene. He has built up a fabulous collection of old racing machines and is a very hard man to beat in classic bike races.

World Champion: 500 cc 1956, 1958, 1959 & 1960.   350 cc 1958, 1959 & 1960

Below: Artie Bell: an horrific crash in the 1950 Belgian Grand Prix cut short the career of this charismatic Ulsterman, leader of the Norton team.

Right: Reg Armstrong: well-educated Dubliner who was second string to Geoff Duke, first at Norton and later at Gilera.

Top: Ercole Frigerio: Gilera-supported sidecar competitor who finished runner-up to Eric Oliver three years in succession. Fatally injured in a crash at the Swiss Grand Prix in 1952.

Above: Hans Haldemann: genial Swiss who successfully campaigned Norton-powered outfits in the early days.

Right: Tommy Wood: scored many successes on home-tuned Moto Guzzis, including second place in the 250 cc World Championship in 1951.

Above left: Ray Amm: brilliant Rhodesian who never gave up. Kept the Norton flag flying until they quit. Killed in his first race for MV Agusta at Imola in 1955. With *(above)* Rod Coleman: ever-smiling, balding New Zealander who led the AJS team in 1953 and 1954.

Below: Walter Zeller: wealthy Bavarian who raced with great success for BMW – but the bikes were never quite fast enough.

Above: Sammy Miller: before he established himself as one of the best trials riders of all time, Irish-born Sammy was a brilliant road racer who made his name on Norton and NSU machines. Later raced for Mondial, Ducati and CZ.

Right: Ken Kavanagh: dwarflike Australian who rode second string to Ray Amm in the Norton team and later switched to Moto Guzzi. Now lives in Italy.

Right: Bob McIntyre: dour but brilliant Scot who did the double for Gilera at the Golden Jubilee TT in 1957 (including the first-ever lap of the Isle of Man at over 100 mph) but who never had much luck on the continent. Lost his life in a crash at Oulton Park.

Below: Bob Brown: yet another Australian who made it to the top – first on Nortons and then, in 1957, on works Gileras. Killed when he crashed on a works Honda practising for the German Grand Prix at Solitude in 1960.

Below: John Hartle: a former Royal Signals despatch rider, he starred for Norton and MV Agusta and raced works Gileras for the Scuderia Duke in 1963. Fatally injured in a crash at Scarborough.

Above: Dickie Dale: made his name on a variety of machines before joining MV Agusta and later Moto Guzzi. Lost his life at the Nürburgring.

THE SIXTIES

Giacomo Agostini (MV Agusta) leads Mike Hailwood (Honda) during their epic battle in the 500 cc class of the 1967 Dutch TT. Hailwood won this race but the Italian took the championship.

By MICK WOOLLETT

BY rights, Mike Hailwood's early rivals should have hated the slim, shy teenager from Nettlebed near Oxford, for his brash millionaire father Stan, boss of the Kings of Oxford motor cycle empire, did everything in his power to buy success for his only son.

Yet Mike was so different from his father and such an obviously nice guy that he was very soon accepted as one of the boys. However, without his father constantly pushing, and providing the best machines prepared by the top tuners, Mike would not have succeeded as he did: he was far too easy-going and not in the least mechanically minded.

Together, though – and it was surely a chance in several million – they made the perfect team. Mike was not only a naturally brilliant rider but he had the gift of being able to get the best out of whatever machine he got

Man in a hurry. Mike Hailwood in action on a six-cylinder Honda during the 1967 250 cc Belgian Grand Prix.

his leg across – he was, quite simply, the best motor cycle racer of all time.

He first appeared on the scene as a 17-year-old novice on a 125 cc MV Agusta in 1957. That winter he went racing in South Africa to sharpen his talents and in 1958 contested all four classes of the British championships and won three of them! A year later he went one better by making a clean sweep of all four and winning his first classic – the 125 cc class of the Ulster on a Ducati.

The sheer stamina and skill that it took to get the best out of four different bikes at a single meeting was mind-boggling – as I found out when Stan invited me to Brands Hatch to try the winning machines. They were a 125 cc Ducati, a 250 cc Mondial and a pair of Nortons for the 350 cc and 500 cc classes – all highly tuned four-strokes and – as I discovered when I missed a gear on the 500 and bent a valve – all with their own limitations and idiosyncrasies.

Yet such was Mike's talent that he was able to switch from one to the other as many as 16 times in a single day to complete practice sessions, semi-finals and finals – often winning the lot!

In 1961 he came within a few miles of winning all four Isle of Man TTs – taking the 125 cc and 250 cc on Hondas and the Senior on a Norton; his AJS 7R let him down when he was leading the Junior, when the crankpin broke on the last lap. He went on to win his first World Championship, the 250 cc, for Honda, and at the end of that year joined MV Agusta.

After winning four 500 cc titles in succession for the Italians he switched to the Honda team for 1966 and did the 250/350 double twice, to bring his tally to nine world titles before the Japanese factory pulled out at the end of 1967. After a year racing in non-classic events Mike switched to cars, but a major shunt cut short a promising career and he 'retired' to New Zealand.

The story is not over yet. After a couple of minor outings on bikes Hailwood returned, out of the blue, for the 1978 TT. With Martini backing he won the Formula One event on a Ducati with a record lap of over 110 mph – and in 1979 he popped up again, aged 39 and with even less hair, to race a works four-cylinder two-stroke Suzuki in the Senior TT.

It seemed an absurd thing to do – to try to master yet another machine, this time a 170 mph Grand Prix two-stroke, around the world's most unforgiving circuit. Typically of the man he succeeded, brilliantly. He not only won the race but set a new lap record of 114.02 mph.

Ironically he was killed when nipping out to buy fish and chips: a truck driver did a U-turn across a dual carriageway in front of his car, in 1981.

World Champion: 500 cc 1962, 1963, 1964 & 1965

World Champion: 350 cc 1966 & 1967.   250 cc 1961, 1966 & 1967

WHEN 20-year-old Gary Hocking arrived in Europe in June 1958 he had no bikes, no transport – and very little money. But luckily he had good friends. Jim Redman lent him his spare 350 cc Norton and English sponsor Reg Dearden equipped him with a 500 cc Norton and found him an old V8 Ford van.

Known to his friends by his schoolboy nickname 'Socks', Gary was an immediate front-runner. He made his European début at the Dutch TT and finished sixth in the 500 cc race. The next week he won both classes at an international race at Piestany, Czechoslovakia.

A few weeks later the quiet Rhodesian, who had learned all his racing on the southern Africa tracks, rocked the establishment when he finished third in the 500 cc class of the German Grand Prix on the ultra-tricky Nürburgring – beaten only by the works MV Agustas and ahead of all the local aces who knew every inch of the circuit.

This obvious natural talent soon attracted works attention and in 1959 Hocking won the 250 cc Swedish and Ulster Grands Prix on factory MZ two-strokes and so impressed MV Agusta that they immediately signed him for 1960. He responded by finishing second in both the 125 cc and 250 cc classes behind team-mate Carlo Ubbiali – and he was also runner-up to John Surtees in the 350 cc division.

When Surtees retired Hocking took over as top man at MV Agusta and won both the 350 cc and 500 cc World Championships in 1961. But by '62 his interest was flagging and, after the death of his close friend Tom Phillis in the Isle of Man that year, he sensationally retired in mid-season.

A few weeks later he flew back to Europe to have a crack at car racing. He was so successful that Rob Walker signed him to replace Stirling Moss in his équipe. Ironically Gary was killed driving a Lotus V8 in a race near Durban in December 1962.

World Champion: 500 cc 1961.   350 cc 1961

A quiet, wry smile and a dry sense of humour were the trademarks of Tom Phillis, yet another of the small band of Commonwealth riders who have made good on European circuits.

Born in Sydney in 1934, he started racing on a 350 cc Velocette 20 years later and, after gaining experience in Australia, he set out for Europe in 1958 and was an immediate success, winning both the 350 cc and 500 cc classes at Thruxton on a pair of Manx Nortons that he'd prepared himself.

He said later that he based his style on that of fellow-Aussies Jack Ahearn and Maurice Quincey – trying to blend Ahearn's aggression with Quincey's ease of riding and neatness. He succeeded and by the time Honda arrived on the scene at the 1959 Isle of Man TT, Tom was among the top private riders.

Although the Hondas were not fast Tom was impressed, and during the next winter he wrote to the factory and asked to be considered for a ride in 1960. Honda responded by offering him bikes for the TT; in June that year the Australian became the first western professional to race a factory Honda.

There was no happy ending. The bikes were still no match for the European machines and Phillis eventually limped home tenth in the 125 cc race. The 250 cc was more competitive and he was lying fourth until gearbox trouble put him out. Gradually Honda sorted the bikes out and in 1961 Phillis was the victor in a nail-biting battle for the 125 cc World Championship that went to the final round in Argentina, where he won the race and snatched the crown from Ernst Degner (MZ and EMC). Phillis also finished second in the 250 cc table that year, beaten only by Mike Hailwood (Honda).

After another successful season back home in Australia Tom, wife Betty and their two children Debbie and Tom junior returned for 1962 and it was while racing the new 285 cc Honda in the 350 cc Junior TT that Tom met his death, crashing at Laurel Bank.

VARIETY has been the spice of Hugh Anderson's motor cycle racing career. Born in Auckland, New Zealand, in 1936 he was first a road racer, then a top class motocross rider and now, in his mid-50s, he campaigns an immaculate 500 cc G50 Matchless in classic bike events all over the world.

He started out on the two-wheel trail in his native New Zealand. There he rode in a variety of events before setting out, in 1960, for what was then the Mecca of the motor cycle racing world – the Isle of Man. Racing a new 7R AJS and a 500 cc Manx Norton he had no luck, but a string of steady placings on the continent, together with occasional wins at lesser events (notably Madrid), proved that he was competitive.

His 1961 season was interrupted by a heavy crash in the 350 cc race at the Dutch TT while he was dicing with Ernesto Brambilla on a works Bianchi twin for fourth place. He broke a few bones but it turned out to be a lucky 'break' for, in story-book style, he fell in love with his Dutch nurse and married her.

Back in action he caught the eye of the Suzuki team and scored his first successes for them in the East German Grand Prix at the Sachsenring in 1962 when he finished third in the then-new 50 cc class. Steady rides on the 125 cc Suzuki, including a win in the poorly supported Argentine Grand Prix, meant that he kept his place in the Suzuki line-up for 1963.

That year the Suzukis really flew, and they carried the slim Kiwi to World Championship honours in both the 50 cc and 125 cc classes. He won the tiddler title again the next year, and the 125 cc for a second time in 1965. He stayed with Suzuki in 1966 but, concerned at the high accident rate among riders, he quit at the end of that season to race in motocross events and run a motor cycle business in Assen, home of the Dutch TT and of his wife. Later they moved to New Zealand.

World Champion: 125 cc 1963 & 1965.   50 cc 1963 & 1964

ALTHOUGH he only ever won a single World Championship, the 50 cc for Suzuki in 1962, Ernst Degner was involved in the greatest cloak-and-dagger drama ever to hit motor cycle racing, a real-life story to equal any fiction.

It happened in 1961. At that time the pallid East German with the sparkling blue eyes was the star of the East German MZ team: the previous year he had finished third behind the works MV Agustas in the 125 cc class. When the teams went to Sweden for the penultimate round of the 1961 championship, Ernst was leading by two points from Tom Phillis (Honda).

But Degner's mind was on other things. He had laid careful plans to get his family out of East Germany while he was in Sweden, and to defect himself immediately after the race. He actually led, and looked to have the World Championship in the bag, until the MZ stopped with mechanical problems.

Ernst retired out on the course, walked to the pits, took his car and drove to join his family who had crossed to West Germany in a furniture van. But the drama of the 125 cc class was not over. Tom Phillis took the lead when Degner retired and looked set to clinch the title. Then he too retired – which meant that both had to go to Argentina for the final race.

Obviously Degner had no machine so Joe Ehrlich took him under his wing and lent him one of his potent EMC two-strokes that Mike Hailwood and Phil Read had campaigned that year. Unfortunately for Ernst there were all sorts of problems and the title slipped away.

Degner then joined Suzuki and had a big hand in helping to design their new racing machines. He was rewarded with the 50 cc championship and, after retiring, he came to England to work for Joe Ehrlich before returning to live in West Germany.

THERE is no doubt about it – racing changed Jim Redman. When he first came over from Rhodesia, early in 1958, he was a carefree character who made friends easily. But when he quit the racing scene, after sustaining a shoulder injury in the 1966 Belgian Grand Prix, he was a disappointed man who had few real pals.

Mind you, his upbringing was tough. Born in Hampstead, his father and mother died within months of one another when Jim, working in a London garage, was just 16. He and his slightly older sister, Jackie, were left to bring up their 11-year-old twin brother and sister.

With National Service looming Jim skipped the country and went to Rhodesia. There he established a home, where he was soon joined by the rest of the family. He started racing on a Triumph twin loaned to him by John Love and later the two of them began a motor cycle business in Bulawayo.

After racing all over southern Africa, winning the South African 350 cc title on a 7R AJS, Jim sailed for Europe and was immediately successful. In his very first meeting, at Brands Hatch early in 1958, he finished second in the main event, beaten only by Derek Minter, the acknowledged master of the Kent circuit.

Racing Nortons he was always in the hunt, but there were a lot of good young riders about in those days and Jim had to wait until June 1960 for his chance. It came when Tom Phillis crashed during practice for the Dutch TT. Jim was one of several in line to take over, but Tom put in a good word, Jim got the Honda ride and he finished fourth in the 125 cc race – a good performance by a big man.

Soon Jim was racing the 250 cc, a bike far more suited to his size, and he finished second in the final Grand Prix, the Italian at Monza. He raced the two lightweight classes for Honda the following year, establishing and improving his status in the Honda camp until, in 1962, he was virtually running the team. His strong personality and will to succeed impressed the hesitant Japanese.

In 1962 Redman concentrated on the 250 cc and 350 cc classes, winning the World Championship in the smaller class for two years in succession and the 350 cc title for fours years in a row. Having made a lot of money, his one remaining racing ambition was to crown his career by taking the 500 cc title.

Honda produced a bike for the big class in 1966, when Jim was joined by Mike Hailwood. It was agreed that Jim was to take the 500 cc title, if he could, while Mike had a free hand in the 250 and 350 divisions. But Redman found the going tough, up against the dashing young Giacomo Agostini on the new three-cylinder MV Agusta, and he crashed in the rain while trying to beat the Italian in the Belgian Grand Prix.

Redman retired to live in South Africa, where he set up a time-share country club. He later became involved in pyramid selling and made a brief visit to England just before the practice was outlawed in the UK. He now lives in a splendid house in Durban where his main interests are horse racing and helping his younger son with his motocross bikes.

German Grand Prix 1962 and Jim Redman (Honda) leads team-mate Bob McIntyre during the 250 cc race. They finished first and second.

World Champion: 350 cc 1962, 1963, 1964 & 1965.   250 cc 1962 & 1963

TALL, blond and with light blue eyes Max Deubel cut a typically German figure – and his Teutonic attention to detail, allied to cool, skilful riding made him and his passenger Emil Horner the most successful sidecar team of the 1960s.

After making his mark in German junior races Deubel first contested the World Championships in 1960. With another passenger he did sufficiently well to persuade BMW to back him with factory-prepared engines for the 1961 season – and it was then that Emil Horner, a short, cheerful character who had previously ridden with the one-legged Alwin Ritter, joined him.

They never looked back. With both 1960 champion Helmut Fath and the dashing Swiss, Florian Camathias, out of action with serious injuries, the German pairing battled it out with another Swiss, Fritz Scheidegger, to win the 1961 World Championship.

They repeated the dose in 1962, beating Camathias, and came out on top again the following year when the championship developed into a three-cornered fight between the two Swiss and Deubel/Horner. Just two points separated the trio at the end of the season.

The German duo won the title for a fourth time in 1964, equalling the record set by Eric Oliver, but Scheidegger eventually got the better of them in 1965 and, after one more unsuccessful attempt to regain the crown, Deubel and Horner retired at the end of the 1966 season.

It says much for his cool temperament and skilful machine preparation that Deubel never had a serious accident during his career. He now runs the family hotel in the country village of Muhlenau, a few miles to the east of Cologne, and like compatriot and fellow sidecar champion Willi Noll he serves the sport as an official of the FIM.

Sidecar wheel inches in the air, rear wheel drifting – Helmut Fath, assisted by passenger Wolfgang Kalauch, powers his four-cylinder URS to victory in the 1969 Belgian Grand Prix. They averaged 111.79 mph.

N O man has devoted more time to racing and the building and preparation of racing motor cycles than Helmut Fath. For over 30 years he has slaved away in his workshop in the forest just outside Heidelberg, perfecting first a special BMW-based engine, then a one-off four-cylinder unit designed to defeat the all-conquering BMWs in the sidecar class, and now preparing two-strokes.

I first met Helmut at Chimay in Belgium in 1956, when I was passengering Cyril Smith. We were leading the race on the last lap when we slowed with mechanical problems. Half a mile from the finish I looked back and there was Helmut on his BMW, coming up so fast that I knew he must overtake us and win.

But he did not. He sat behind to the finish. At the time I thought he must have struck trouble too. As a young German it would have been an enormous feather in his cap to have beaten the former British World Champion.

Years later I asked him what the problem had been. 'Oh, no trouble. It just didn't seem right for me to take advantage of Cyril's problems. To me he was the winner,' he replied in his gravelly voice.

Competing against the official BMW teams he perfected his own fuel-injected BMW and won the 1960 Sidecar World Championship. Success was followed by tragedy, for the next year Fath was involved in an accident at the Nürburgring in which he was very seriously injured and his passenger and friend Alfred Wohlgemuth was killed.

During his long convalescence he worked with Peter Kuhn, a young doctor of engineering, to design and build a completely original double overhead camshaft four-cylinder racing engine. Using this he returned to racing to win the 1968 World Championship and, after he had retired, to sponsor Horst Owesle to the championship three years later.

In recent years he has turned his talents to tuning two-strokes for solo riders – still using his little workshop in the forest.

World Champion: Sidecars 1960 & 1968

ARD to believe that, as I write, Luigi Taveri is 60 years old. Like Geoff Duke he seems to have weathered the years better than most. And with his black, crinkly hair and small, slim figure he still looks every inch the professional racer when he pulls on his leathers and that famous red helmet at today's classic bike events.

Born near Zurich, where he now runs a very upmarket car crash repair business, he started his racing career as passenger to elder brother Hans in the 1947 Swiss Grand Prix. A year later he went solo and one of his early mounts was a pre-war Swedish 500 cc Husqvarna vee-twin.

He rode machines from various manufacturers, including Parilla, BMW, Moto Guzzi, Velocette, AJS and Norton, and won several Swiss championships – with occasional sidecar outings until as late as 1954 when he passengered Hans Haldemann to sixth place in the Swiss Grand Prix. Late that year Nello Pagani invited him to ride works 500 cc MV Agustas at the end of season meetings.

Signed by MV Agusta for 1955 he won Grands Prix in both the 125 cc and 250 cc classes and he continued with the Italian factory, though always in the shadow of Carlo Ubbiali and Tarquinio Provini. He broke with MV Agusta in 1959 when he raced MZ and Ducati machines, but he rejoined them for 1960.

That year he saw the potential of the beautifully engineered but slower Honda works machines and in 1961 he switched to the Japanese bikes. It was an association that was to last until he retired as reigning 125 cc World Champion at the end of the 1966 season.

During his years with Honda he won 26 Grands Prix and three 125 cc world titles, using three different Honda machines – first a twin, then a four, and finally the incredible five-cylinder that revved to 20,000!

T HE crowds loved Bill Ivy. His devil-may-care, let's have a crack at it attitude somehow transmitted itself from the charismatic little man from Maidstone to the thousands who lined the circuits.

Born in 1942, he started work as a trainee mechanic at Chisholm Brothers, a motor cycle dealers in Maidstone, when he left school. And he started racing on a tiny two-stroke 50 cc Itom, tuned and sponsored by Chisholm, in 1959.

A succession of bikes and sponsors followed as Bill raced Bultacos and Yamahas for Barry Sheene's father, Frank, a 250 cc Cotton, a 125 cc Honda for Chisholm, on which he won the British championship in 1964, and a variety of bigger bikes for dealer Geoff Monty. Eventually he joined the most professional non-factory team of the time, run by 'Uncle' Tom Kirby, a Hornchurch dealer. This caused a bit of a stink because Bill made the switch from Geoff Monty's bikes to Tom's without warning, just after Easter 1965 – but he felt he had to seize the opportunity if he was to progress.

He got his first works ride with Yamaha in 1965, finishing seventh in the 125 cc TT and fourth in Holland and Japan – where he also impressed by finishing third in the 250 cc race. It was enough to get him promoted into the team for 1966.

Little Bill, who shared a flat with Mike Hailwood at Heston, near London airport, at this time, responded by finishing second in the 125 cc World Championship – and then by winning it in 1967. And he proved just how good he was on the 250 cc by coming a very close third to Hailwood and team-mate Read in the 250 cc class.

After a disastrous 1968 season, in which he lost out to Read, Bill split his time in 1969 between racing cars and riding the new four-cylinder 350 cc two-stroke Jawa in the World Championship. He pushed Agostini hard in both Germany and Holland, but then lost his life while practising on the Jawa for the East German Grand Prix in July that year.

I T was a long haul but Switzerland's Fritz Scheidegger, with John Robinson from Purley in the chair, finally got the better of the German BMW boys to win the Sidecar World Championship in 1965 – the first time a non-German had taken the title since Eric Oliver in 1953!

Looking more like a farmer than a speedster, the tall, slim Swiss with the steel-framed spectacles grew up in the little village of Langenthal where he was born in 1930. Mechanically minded, he worked in the local motor cycle shop and started racing at grass track events in 1950 on a 350 cc BSA Gold Star.

For seven years he mixed grass track and road racing, solo and sidecar, and won several Swiss championships – including the sidecar title three years in succession. Towards the end of the 1957 season near-neighbour Edgar Strub, already an established international, rang him. Edgar had entered a meeting in San Sebastian, Spain, but could not make it – would Scheidegger like to take over the entry?

Fitting road tyres to his grass track Norton he set off. It was no fairy-tale début – he retired with engine trouble – but the seed had been sown and, within days, he had bought a competitive BMW outfit from yet another Swiss, Florian Camathias. And a couple of weeks later he scored his first championship points when he came third in the Italian Grand Prix at Monza – his third road race.

After that it was a long, hard struggle to get right to the top. Third place in the championship in 1959 was followed by runner-up spot the next year – and again in 1961. There were further third places in 1962 and 1963, and in 1964 he ran Max Deubel very close to claim runner-up spot yet again.

His persistence was rewarded, for BMW finally relented and loaned him works engines. These, together with the low kneeler outfit which he built himself, allied to his skill and determination, gave him the edge and he ousted Deubel to win the title in 1965 and again in 1966. But there was to be no hat-trick: a crash in an early season meeting at Mallory Park cost him his life in March 1967.

SIX times winner of the Sidecar World Championship, little Klaus Enders is the most successful three-wheeled racer of all time. Yet he achieved his successes so smoothly, so discreetly (if you can use such a term about motor sport) that you hardly hear his name mentioned when all-time sidecar greats are discussed.

To Klaus racing was a science. He went as fast as he could but he never took reckless chances – there would always be another race. He first got among the Grand Prix results at the 1966 TT when he finished fourth and won the award for the 'Best Newcomer'. A fourth in Holland followed and in 1967 he took over when Max Deubel retired and Fritz Scheidegger was killed.

During 1968 he had to give way to a rejuvenated Helmut Fath on his new, home-built, four-cylinder URS – but with BMW backing Enders and passenger Ralf Engelhardt were back on top in 1969. The following year Wolfgang Kalauch replaced Engelhardt in the chair but Enders went on winning – and at the end of the year he 'retired'.

But after a year driving BMW cars he returned to sidecar racing, encouraged by Dieter Busch who built his engines and the Munich factory which had lost the three-wheeler crown to Owesle and his four-cylinder Fath-inspired URS machine in 1971. With Ralf Engelhardt back in the chair Enders won the title in 1972, 1973 and 1974 to bring his tally to that record-breaking six.

Born at Giessen near Frankfurt in 1937 he had actually started racing in 1960 at the Norisring circuit, scene of Hitler's mammoth pre-war Nürnberg rallies. For a while he raced both solos and sidecars, and in 1963 won the German junior solo title on a Manx Norton. He now lives in Wetzlar.

World Champion: Sidecars 1967, 1969, 1970, 1972, 1973 & 1974

PHIL READ

Left: **Heavyweight championship! Phil Read (MV Agusta) and Giacomo Agostini (Yamaha) slug it out during the 1975 German Grand Prix at Hockenheim.**

Below left: **Heading for yet another win – Phil Read on his 250 cc Yamaha at the French Grand Prix, Clermont-Ferrand, in 1972.**

RAISED in Luton in a strictly middle-class suburban area overlooking the famous Vauxhall factory, Phil Read ranks very close to Mike Hailwood both for skill and an inborn talent for getting the best out of every bike he got his leg over. And during a career which spanned an incredible 27 seasons he raced a wider variety of factory machines than any other professional.

Born in 1939, he started racing on a 350 cc BSA in 1956 when he was an apprentice engineer. His mother, a keen motor cyclist, actively encouraged him. He made a winning début in the Isle of Man in 1961 when he won the 350 cc Junior TT on a Norton – the same year that Hailwood won the Senior. It was the start of an intense rivalry that was to end at the 1978 TT!

Early in 1963 Read got his chance. That was the year that Geoff Duke resurrected 1957 Gileras in the 500 cc

class under the Scuderia Duke banner – and first choice Derek Minter was injured early in the season. Duke immediately signed Read to team with John Hartle, and Phil responded brilliantly with third place in the TT and second places in the Dutch and Belgian. A crash in Ulster then put him out, but he had done enough to impress Yamaha.

They gave him a try-out at the Japanese Grand Prix at the end of 1963, where he finished a creditable third. It was the start of a fruitful liaison that ended acrimoniously in 1968.

First, Read beat Redman and Honda to take 250 cc honours in 1964 – a success he repeated the following year. In 1966 he was beaten into second place by Hailwood, who had joined Honda – and in 1967 he fought out a furious battle with 'Mike the Bike' that ended with them tied on points, Hailwood taking the title because he had more outright wins.

In 1968 he had his equally famous grudge match with team-mate Bill Ivy when, defying team orders, he cunningly outwitted the Japanese and Ivy to win both 125 cc and 250 cc titles.

With the works teams pulling out Phil campaigned his own machines and, in 1971, won the 250 cc title for the fourth time riding his own twin-cylinder Yamaha tuned by German Helmut Fath, the former sidecar title-holder. That year 'Speedy' travelled by Rolls Royce, putting on the style that perhaps attracted the attention of MV Agusta.

Whatever it was, and Read can be a charming and persuasive talker, he joined the Italians as second string to Giacomo Agostini – only Phil had no intention of playing second fiddle to anyone. To everyone's amazement he ousted the Italian, who had won the title for the previous seven years in succession, from the top of the 500 cc tree.

Agostini left MV Agusta to join Yamaha for a head-to-head confrontation in 1974 – but again Read beat him, to clinch his seventh World Championship. The Italian finally gained revenge in 1975 when Read finished second, quitting MV Agusta at the end of the season.

The following year he raced a Suzuki in the 500 cc class, but age was catching him up and at the end of the season he announced his retirement. However, he made a sensational comeback to the TT in 1977 – sensational first because he had openly criticised the Isle of Man as being 'too dangerous' and second because he won the Senior TT on a works Suzuki and the Formula One race on a factory Honda.

Phil returned to the Isle of Man in 1978 to race the big Honda against Mike Hailwood (Ducati) in the Formula One event. He retired with an oil leak when lying second. The Island was also the scene of his last race, in 1982.

Now living in Surrey and a keen pilot, Phil still pops up at motor cycle events from time to time.

World Champion: 500 cc 1973 & 1974.   250 cc 1964, 1965, 1968 & 1971.   125 cc 1968

KEL CARRUTHERS

A latecomer to Europe, Kel Carruthers has been involved in racing practically all his life – and although he is now in his early 50s, he is still at every Grand Prix as head mechanical honcho of the Marlboro Yamaha team.

Born in 1938, the only child of a Sydney motor cycle dealer, he grew up amid bikes and was racing by the time he was 16. For several years he was happy to compete locally – then along came Honda. They sent one of a batch of four-cylinder 250 cc racers to Australia and the local importer got Kel to ride it.

For five years he dominated Australian racing with the Honda and a 500 cc Norton and then, early in 1966, he sold up and came to Europe with his wife, Jan, their two children and his father, Jack.

It was tougher than he expected but after a year he started to place regularly on a 350 cc Aermacchi. The factory were impressed and offered him works bikes for 1968 – and the following year came the big break when he switched to Benelli to ride their beautiful little four-cylinder machine in the 250 cc series. On it he came through to win the World Championship at the final round, the Yugoslav Grand Prix. With Benelli pulling out he defended his title on a Yamaha, finishing second to Rod Gould.

By this time he had set up home in California. He had realised that the booming American market offered new opportunities when he raced at Daytona in 1970. With backing from San Diego dealer and record-breaker Don Vesco, Kel and family moved to the States and he finished his racing career there before joining Yamaha to assist with the development of racing machines – a job he has been doing ever since.

World Champion: 250 cc 1969

PATIENCE, outstanding mechanical ability, riding skill and a father who worked for British Airways and had a knack of getting hold of racing machines in Japan combined to put Dave Simmonds on the 125 cc World Championship rostrum at the end of the 1969 season.

Tall, dark and good looking, Dave was brought up in Ashford, Middlesex within a mile of the southern perimeter of London's Heathrow airport where his father worked.

He started his career in 1962 on a pair of Nortons but soon switched to the lightweight classes, assisted by his father who managed to import a rare and speedy ex-works Tohatsu. With this bike Dave won the 125 cc British championship in 1963; and two years later he took the British 250 cc title on another import – a Honda twin.

An ex-works disc-valve 125 cc Kawasaki was soon winging its way from Japan. The bike had been built in 1966 but had made no impact. However, Dave realised that with the works teams out of the class and with the formula now restricted to twin cylinders, the seemingly obsolete 'Kwacker' was in with a chance.

After painstakingly rebuilding the machine Dave took it to the 1968 Italian Grand Prix at the ultra-quick Monza circuit. There he proved the machine's reliability by finishing fourth, and after a further winter's work he set out on the championship trail in 1969.

His achievements surprised even himself. He won eight of the eleven rounds and was the clear-cut champion. Unfortunately the bike was not quick enough to defend the title successfully and, in any case, Dave was switching his attention to the 500 cc class in which he raced a special with Reynolds frame and Kawasaki engine.

He married Julie Boddice, daughter of sidecar racer Bill, and moved north to Kingswinford. He lost his life fighting a caravan fire at a minor meeting at Rungis, Paris in October 1972. Ironically it was not his own caravan – typically, he was helping a friend.

I S it just chance that motor cycle racing's two greatest champions – Mike Hailwood and Giacomo Agostini – have both been the sons of very wealthy fathers? The Hailwood income came from a chain of motor cycle shops; the Agostini fortune from a ferry company that served the northern Italian Lake d'Iseo near Brescia, where Giacomo was born in 1942.

Unlike Stan Hailwood, who did everything he could to encourage Mike, Giacomo's family tried desperately to stop his two-wheeled career; his father even tried to bribe him with the offer of a brand-new sports car if only he would stop.

Quietly determined, Agostini stole away to race without his parents' knowledge, first in hill-climbs, then in junior road race events. His mount was a 175 cc Morini and on it he won his first major series, the 1963 Italian championship for 175 cc sports machines.

End of an era. Giacomo Agostini (MV Agusta) on his way to victory in the 500 cc class of the German Grand Prix at the Nürburgring in 1976. This was the last time that a World Championship race was won by a four-stroke engine.

The quiet, dashingly handsome youngster impressed Alfonso Morini. So when Tarquinio Provini left for Benelli he was the natural replacement to ride the factory's super-fast single-cylinder 250 cc racer.

Despite massive Japanese works opposition, Giacomo took fourth place in the Italian Grand Prix in 1964 and won the 250 cc Italian championship. Never slow to spot an up-and-coming rider, Count Domenico Agusta signed him for the 1965 season to team with that other rich man's son, Mike Hailwood.

At the end of that year Hailwood left to join Honda and, with his apprenticeship served, Agostini, by this time riding the brilliantly engineered three-cylinder, four-stroke MV Agusta, took over with a vengeance. He won the 500 cc World Championship for seven years in succession (1966 to 1972 inclusive) and the 350 cc for another seven (1968 to 1974 inclusive – the last year on a Yamaha). Both are records – and likely to remain so!

True, the opposition at that time was, once Honda had faded from the scene, often mediocre. But it is still a formidable record and Agostini's race wins included ten Isle of Man TT races. In fact, his spectacular riding in the Island, especially the 120 mph wheelie he performed over the bumps at the bottom of Bray Hill, proved him to be not only talented but also completely fearless.

All good things come to an end, however, and Agostini split with MV Agusta at the end of the 1973 season. He switched to Yamaha and made an impressive début when he won, first time out, on the new TZ750 Yamaha at the Daytona 200. Back in Europe he took the 350 cc crown for Yamaha, although he again failed to beat Phil Read in the 500 cc. A year later he had his revenge, beating Read and winning his fifteenth and final World Championship on a 500 cc factory Yamaha.

Agostini continued to race for three more seasons, first for MV Agusta, then on RG500 Suzukis, and finally back to Yamahas for the 1977 season. He scored occasional victories – notably a last Grand Prix win for MV Agusta at a wet German Grand Prix at the Nürburgring in 1976 – but the old consistency had gone.

Always helpful and speaking better and better English as the years go by, Giacomo will be remembered as a gentleman on and off the track. He now lives in a luxurious house at Lovere overlooking Lake d'Iseo, when he's not away managing the Marlboro Yamaha team.

World Champion: 500 cc 1966, 1967, 1968, 1969, 1970, 1971, 1972 & 1975

World Champion: 350 cc 1968, 1969, 1970, 1971, 1972, 1973 & 1974

RALPH BRYANS

ULSTER-born, though now living in Scotland, he won the 50 cc world title in 1965 on a factory Honda and was twice runner-up in the tiddler class, in 1964 and 1966. Also finished third in the 125 cc table in 1966 and third in the 350 cc championship the next year. Reliable and easy-going – an ideal second-string teamster.

World Champion: 50 cc 1965

HANS-GEORG ANSCHEIDT

A 50 cc specialist, he made his name on German-built Kreidler machines before switching to works Suzukis on which he won the 50 cc title three years in succession – 1966 to 1968 inclusive. Born in East Prussia (now part of Poland) he was a studious, quiet man with a sound mechanical background which helped him to get the best out of the technically advanced Suzukis – twin cylinders and a 14-speed gearbox!

World Champion: 50 cc 1966, 1967 & 1968

Alan Shepherd: made his name racing AJS and Matchless machines, taking second place in the 500 cc World Championship in 1962 and 1963, but best remembered for some outstanding rides on the factory East German MZ two-strokes.

Edgar Strub: Swiss hard man who built his own outfits and prepared his own engines – first Norton and then BMW. Finished third in the 1961 sidecar championship at the age of 43. Now lives in Spain.

Tommy Robb: from Belfast, though he later moved to England,
Tommy raced for 22 years, first on the rough, but mainly on the
road. Was signed by Honda in 1962 when he finished third in the
125 cc table and was runner-up in the 350 cc. Switched to Yamaha
and retired after finishing fourth on a Seeley in the 1970
500 cc championship.

Gyula Marsovszky: left Hungary during the 1956 uprising and settled in Switzerland. Scored many successes on a 500 cc Matchless before he was runner-up in the 500 cc class on an Italian-built Linto in 1969. Later he raced Yamahas.

Mike Duff: one of the few Canadians to star in Europe, Mike raced AJS and Matchless machines so successfully that he was recruited by Yamaha to team with Phil Read. Later had a sex-change operation and now lives in Canada as a woman.

Florian Camathias: a charming Swiss who looked like a solicitor but was a tiger once the flag dropped. Was four-times runner-up in the sidecar class (1958, 1959, 1962 and 1963) before he lost his life at Brands Hatch late in 1965.

Georg Auerbacher: dedicated, cheerful German who raced BMWs and was three times runner-up in the sidecar championship (1967, 1968 and 1970). Was very seriously injure in the Isle of Man.

Frank Perris: always immaculate, he scored his first successes on AJS and Matchless machines but switched to Norton to finish third in the 1961 500 cc championship. Was recruited by Suzuki and was runner-up to team-mate Hugh Anderson in the 1965 125 cc championship.

Above: Colin Seeley: a motor cycle dealer and later manufacturer of Seeley racing machines, Colin learned the three-wheel trade on a Matchless-powered outfit but switched to BMW to finish third in the table in 1964 and 1966.

Paddy Driver: South African-born, Paddy came over with Jim Redman in 1958. Made a name on Nortons and had a brief spell with Suzuki before their machines were competitive. Switched to AJS/Matchless and finished third in the 500 cc championship in 1965. Retired to his Johannesburg home but continued to race on four wheels well into his 50s.

Jack Ahearn: rough, tough and with a heart of gold, Jack enjoyed life to the full. He came over from Australia in 1954 and campaigned Nortons, finishing second in the 500 cc championship in 1964 when he was 40. Also raced a works 250 cc four-cylinder Suzuki.

Franta Stastny: one of the great characters of the Sixties, Czech Franta raced Jawa factory machines. He won three 350 cc Grands Prix and was runner-up in the championship in 1961. A talented ice-hockey player, he retired to work in Czech television.

Santiago Herrero: yet another talented continental whose career was cut short by a fatal Isle of Man TT crash. Racing the single-cylinder two-stroke works Ossa he won three Grands Prix in 1969 and finished a close third in the championship. He was leading the 1970 title chase before his accident.

Renzo Pasolini: finished third in the 350 cc table on an Aermacchi in 1966, then raced the four-cylinder Benellis, taking runner-up spot in the 350 cc table in 1968. Returned to Aermacchi to race their new two-strokes in 1972 when he placed second and third in the 250/350 cc tables, but lost his life early in 1973 at Monza.

Jack Findlay: first came over from Australia in 1958 – and is still here, living in Paris. Totally dedicated, Jack was the outstanding 'privateer' of the 1960s, finishing third in the 500 cc table in 1966 and second in 1968. Switched from Matchless to Suzuki and raced works bikes for the factory in 1973 and 1974. Won the FIM 750 cc Coupe in 1975 on a Yamaha and finally retired in 1978 at the age of 43.

Champions three: Isle of Man TT winner
Tarquinio Provini (left), Carlo Ubbiali and a
young Mike Hailwood make a relaxed trio after
their 1958 250 cc race.

The 500s line up for the start of the 1958 Belgian Grand Prix at Spa-Francorchamps. The eventual winner, John Surtees *(far right)*, sits on his MV Agusta while Geoff Duke waits calmly on his white BMW (bike number two).

Carlo Ubbiali on his 250 MV Agusta. The dour Italian won three World Championships in this class, but was even more effective on 125s, achieving six titles.

Luigi Taveri (above) and that famous red helmet in action during the 1958 German Grand Prix. Despite occasional victories with MV Agusta lasting success was achieved only after his switch to Honda.

Libero Liberati (left) led the Gilera team to the 1957 500 cc title after number one rider Geoff Duke's challenge was blunted by injuries.

Above: **Giacomo Agostini, the most successful Grand Prix rider of all. As well as 15 World Championships, he took a record 122 race wins in the 350 cc and 500 cc classes. 'Ago' is pictured above on the 500 cc MV Agusta at Bray Hill in the 1970 Isle of Man TT.**

Left: **Mike Hailwood is regarded by many as the greatest of them all. His duels on the Honda with Agostini's MV in the mid-Sixties are legend.**

Phil Read *(left)* **proved to be Agostini's fiercest rival after Hailwood turned his attention to racing cars. Read was not content to play second fiddle at MV Agusta, and ended his team leader's run of seven championships in 1973, retaining the title the following year.**

Agostini *(above)* **moved to Yamaha for 1974 and turned the tables on Read by winning the last of his record eight 500 cc titles in 1975.**

Left: **Jarno Saarinen: a remarkable talent whose death at Monza in 1973 left a huge gap in the sport.**

Above: **Walter Villa campaigned his Harley-Davidson to great effect in the mid-Seventies, winning three consecutive 250 cc titles as well as the 1976 350 cc crown.**

Johnny Cecotto: a shooting star and 350 cc World Champion at his first attempt. The young Venezuelan (left) **failed to maintain this success in the 500 cc class and soon moved on to motor racing.**

Right: **One of the sport's greatest characters, Barry Sheene won the admiration of the British public as much for his struggles to regain fitness following horrendous accidents in 1975 and 1982 as for his 500 cc World Championship successes of 1976 and 1977.**

The immensely gifted Kork Ballington headed the Kawasaki challenge, achieving a 250 cc/350 cc double in both 1978 and 1979. Ultimate success in the 500 class eluded the South African, who moved to the United States where he raced Hondas with distinction.

'King Kenny' led the American assault on the 500 cc title in the late Seventies with a hat-trick of wins for Yamaha in 1978, '79 and '80. After his retirement in the mid-Eighties Roberts (above) concentrated on building a successful racing team of his own.

'The King of the Tiddlers', Angel Nieto (left), on his 1981 125 cc championship-winning Minarelli at the British Grand Prix – the fourth of seven such titles. The little Spaniard had previously amassed another six championships in the 50 cc class.

Veteran German rider Anton Mang *(right)* earned five World Championships in the Eighties – none better than his 1987 250 cc triumph on the Honda, when he won this most competitive of classes decisively.

Above: The 1983 season saw a titanic struggle for the 500 cc championship between Kenny Roberts's Yamaha (seen leading) and Freddie Spencer on the Honda. Both riders won six races, but the title went to Spencer by two points.

Freddie Spencer on the 500 cc Honda. In 1985 he became the only rider to win both the 250 cc and 500 cc titles in the same season. Subsequently beset by injuries and loss of form, Freddie was never to figure in the championship race again.

The view most riders have of four times 500 cc champion Eddie Lawson, certainly the most complete rider of the past decade. His successful switch from Yamaha to Honda merely confirmed his status as one of motor cycle racing's greats.

Left: Wayne Gardner captured his public's imagination in much the same way as Barry Sheene had a decade earlier. Certainly his on-the-limit approach won him fans worldwide as well as a deserved 500 cc championship in 1987.

Spain's Jorge Martinez continued the tradition of Nieto by dominating the smaller classes with his Derbi, while 1989 saw his fellow-countryman Alex Criville *(above)* win the 125 cc class to become the sport's youngest-ever World Champion at only 19 years of age.

The development of the sidecar over three
decades can be clearly seen in these photos of
(top) Helmut Fath's Sixties URS, Rolf Biland
(centre) at speed on the 1978 championship-
winning Yamaha, and the present-day master,
Steve Webster, aboard the LCR-Krauser.

THE SEVENTIES

Yamaha signed Kenny Roberts to lead their 500 cc challenge in 1978. Here Kenny leads Pat Hennen (Suzuki) in the Venezuelan Grand Prix that year.

By MICK WOOLLETT

THE heart was torn out of the 1973 season when Finland's Jarno Saarinen and Renzo Pasolini of Italy were killed in a single accident at the Monza circuit near Milan in late April.

At the time Jarno was virtually unbeatable. Riding factory Yamahas he had already won the Daytona 200 that year, the first-ever European to triumph in America's classic event, and the Imola 200. And when the World Championship events started he was just as dominant, winning the opening three rounds of the 250 cc series and two of the three 500 cc races. He went to Monza for the Italian Grand Prix leading both championship tables – and there he died, victim of an accident caused by others.

Raised in Turku, the Finnish end of the ferry crossing from Sweden, Saarinen was an all-rounder: he had been Finnish ice-racing champion and a speedway ace before concentrating on road racing in 1970.

He had a distinctive flat-on-the-tank style and his bikes sported unusual handlebars which projected down at a 45-degree angle, something like those fitted to the Brooklands racers of the Thirties. Jarno, who spoke excellent English and was always helpful, said that he had better control with those 'bars when his bike started to slide.

A good mechanic, he prepared his own Yamahas in the early days and finished fourth in the 250 cc class that first year. In 1971 he won his first Grand Prix – the 250 cc Spanish at Járama – and moved up to third in the final championship table.

Typically stylish riding from Jarno Saarinen as the little Finn powers his works Yamaha to a win in the 250 cc class of the German Grand Prix at Hockenheim in 1973 – just a few days before his death at Monza.

Yamaha produced new racers with water-cooled engines for 1972 and Saarinen was one of the riders chosen to race them in both the 250 cc and 350 cc classes. He responded brilliantly and, for a while, looked like taking both titles.

In the bigger class he beat Giacomo Agostini on the three-cylinder MV Agusta fair and square in the opening rounds in Germany and France. The Italians responded by bringing out a new four-cylinder machine and by signing Phil Read to support Agostini. Their plan worked. Agostini took the title with Saarinen second, but no one could deny Jarno in the 250 cc division and, fittingly, he clinched the World Championship at the Finnish Grand Prix at Imatra.

When Yamaha decided to field a pukka works team for 1973, and to move into the 500 cc class with a new four-cylinder two-stroke, Saarinen was the first man they signed. And the former university student looked set to rival Hailwood, Read and Agostini as an all-time great – until that fateful day at Monza.

World Champion: 250 cc 1972

SWEDEN'S sole motor cycle road racing World Champion, Kent Andersson only started his competition career after recovering from a serious road accident in which he broke his back. Deciding that riding on the road was too dangerous, the tall, blond Swede bought a 125 cc Bultaco racer. A second place in a local event confirmed his natural talent and set him on the path to two world titles.

That first race was in 1963, when he was 21. Two years later he made his international début at Oulton Park in England, and in 1966 he won his first race outside Sweden, the 250 cc class at Mouscron in Belgium.

The first international successes were achieved on a home-tuned special powered by a modified Husqvarna motocross engine. It was fast enough to earn him a few points in the 1966 250 cc World Championship but it was not until 1969 that he really made his mark.

That year he raced a Maico in the 125 cc class and a Yamaha in the 250 cc, finishing fourth and second respectively in the championship tables. For 1970 Kent was promoted into the Yamaha team, to race 250 cc and 350 cc machines, but it was when the Japanese factory moved back into the 125 cc division in 1972 that Andersson really came into his own.

Despite his near-six-foot height he was at his best on the smaller bike and ran Angel Nieto (Derbi) close for the title. He then took over to win the crown in 1973 and 1974. The next year the new Italian Morbidellis were just too fast, and in 1976 Andersson quit racing. But he stayed with Yamaha, working as a development engineer.

R ED-haired Rod Gould was one of the first to realise the full potential of the TD1C Yamaha engine – a simple-looking two-stroke twin developed by the Japanese factory to power a sports machine designed for the American market.

Raised in Banbury, where he worked for local dealer and former racer Eddie Dow, Rod started racing in 1964 on a brace of Manx Nortons. A good mechanic he was reasonably successful but, like all would-be professional riders at the time, his progress was threatened by the lack of suitable 'over the counter' racing machines.

Rod, one of the sport's deep thinkers, did something about this. He went to America, made contact with Yamaha dealer Don Vesco of San Diego, and brought home a TD1C engine, slotting the engine-gearbox unit into a Spanish Bultaco racing frame.

In 1968 he got among the leaders at a number of 250 cc Grands Prix, notably the Belgian, where he finished third behind the works Yamaha of Phil Read and the factory MZ of Heinz Rosner. His average speed was 115.4 mph and he ended the year in fourth place in the championship table.

There were problems in 1969 but in 1970, riding the new twin-cylinder works Yamahas, he romped away with the 250 cc title. The next year Phil Read pushed him down to second place and in 1972 he slipped to third. Still very much in the hunt, he retired after winning the 250 cc Swedish Grand Prix where he beat his two main rivals – Jarno Saarinen and Renzo Pasolini.

For the next few years he ran the Yamaha racing team from Amsterdam. Then he set up a motor cycle dealership in partnership with Mike Hailwood, which unfortunately failed. Rod now lives near Banbury and runs a company offering promotional goods and packages.

World Champion: 250 cc 1970

HORST OWESLE

DIETER BRAUN

DEDICATED and mechanically talented, he won the 1969 German junior sidecar title using BMW power, then worked with Helmut Fath on building and developing the four-cylinder URS. When Fath retired Owesle took over the URS and, with English passenger Peter Rutterford, sprang a surprise by winning the 1971 Sidecar World Championship.

TALL and slim, he raced in motocross and car events before concentrating full time on road racing. Won the 125 cc title in 1970 on an ex-works Suzuki twin and then in 1973, riding a home-tuned Yamaha against the works machines, he carried off the 250 cc crown.

World Champion: Sidecars 1971

World Champion: 250 cc 1973.   125 cc 1970

JAN DE VRIES

DIMINUTIVE Dutchman who won the 50 cc title for the Dutch-sponsored van Veen Kreidler team in 1971 and again in 1973. Born in 1944, he retired as reigning World Champion at the end of the 1973 season.

World Champion: 50 cc 1971 & 1973

HENK VAN KESSEL

THIS near-six-foot Dutchman had trouble squeezing himself onto a 50 cc racer but, after winning numerous Dutch titles on 50 cc and 125 cc machines, he took over the van Veen Kreidler from de Vries to take the 50 cc World Championship in 1974.

World Champion: 50 cc 1974

ANGEL NIETO

MANY of motor cycle racing's top-flight riders have long careers – but none longer than that of Angel Nieto, the little Spaniard who competed in the World Championships for 23 seasons, winning 90 Grands Prix and 13 world titles. He was the undisputed king of the lightweight 50 cc and 125 cc classes, and the statistics place him second only to Giacomo Agostini when it comes to wins and championships. No wonder Spaniards regard him as a national hero.

Son of a Madrid egg-packer and distributor, Angel started work as an apprentice with a local motor cycle dealer at the age of 12. By the time he was 16 'El Nino' (the kid) was racing a Barcelona-built Derbi – and scoring a fourth in his very first event, at Granada, in 1963.

Barcelona is the centre of the Spanish motor cycle industry and Nieto moved there, working first for Bultaco and then moving to Derbi. Realising his potential, they included him in their team in 1964 and he made his World Championship début in the Spanish Grand Prix, finishing fifth in the 50 cc class.

At that time the Japanese teams were pouring money into the sport and Derbi could not hope to compete. Nieto rode mainly in Spain, racing Ducati four-strokes in the bigger classes and Derbis in 50 cc events.

As the Japanese interest waned so the European factories increased their support: in 1969 I was at the East German Grand Prix to see Nieto and his Derbi team-mates celebrate the win that clinched the first of his World Championships – and the first by a Spanish rider.

Perfectly poised: Angel Nieto aboard his 50 cc Derbi during the 1970 Dutch TT.

The next year he ran away with the 50 cc title and was runner-up in the 125 cc but he was, in those days, very much a win-or-bust character. At one Spanish championship meeting that year he is said to have crashed a total of five times!

Gradually he simmered down, refining his fiery win-at-all-costs style as he gained experience – and the race wins and titles came rolling in. The crowd went wild and invaded the Járama circuit when he clinched the 125 cc crown at the Spanish Grand Prix in 1971, and he scored his only double 50 cc and 125 cc championship success the following year.

For 1973 he was tempted away from Derbi by the Italian Morbidelli factory. It was not a successful move, however, and he returned to Derbi the following year. Unfortunately the Spanish machines proved uncompetitive and for 1975 he joined the successful West German Kreidler team, and won the 50 cc title for them.

Then the Spanish Bultaco factory returned to racing and Nieto 'came home' to win the 50 cc title on their Barcelona machines in 1976 and 1977. After that he concentrated on the 125 cc class, winning five further world titles, two for Minarelli and then three for Garelli.

His last race was the German Grand Prix at the end of the 1986 season, and he looked set to make it a story-book finish. Back on a Derbi, he led the 80 cc class until engine trouble forced him out with just miles to go – a suitably dramatic ending to an incredible career.

Married and with a son, Angel junior, Nieto, typically of the people of Madrid, is somewhat dour and unsmiling by nature. Though short he is stocky and strong, a solid slogger who battled on for nearly a quarter century!

World Champion: 125 cc 1971, 1972, 1979, 1981, 1982, 1983 & 1984

World Champion: 50 cc 1969, 1970, 1972, 1975, 1976 & 1977

NOTHING ever seemed to upset Walter Villa. The charming little Italian from Modena takes a laid-back approach to life and is seldom seen without a smile on his face.

Yet, out on the track, he was always in the thick of it. The culmination of his career was in 1976, when he clinched the 250 cc World Championship for the third year – the first and so far only rider ever to win this class for three years in succession.

One of five brothers, Walter, born in 1943, was involved in motor cycling from his earliest days; he started racing on a Morini when he was 19. Elder brother Francesco was the Italian 125 cc champion at the time, and after he had taken that title four times Walter took over to keep it in the family for a further three years (1966 to 1968). At first he rode a Mondial, then a two-stroke Villa which the brothers had designed and built in their own factory in Modena.

Gaining experience on a 250 cc Montesa (a Villa-designed twin), a Morini, an MV Agusta and anything else he could lay his hands on, Walter, at that time racing a four-cylinder Benelli, was blamed for the horrific accident at Monza in 1973 in which both Jarno Saarinen and Renzo Pasolini lost their lives. (It was oil leaking from the Benelli which was the prime cause of the accident.) Villa himself was seriously hurt in the crash, but recovered to win the 250 cc Italian title that same year on a Yamaha.

Walter got his big chance the next season when he was drafted in to replace Gianfranco Bonera in the Harley-Davidson team, run by the Italian Aermacchi factory which had been bought by the American parent company.

Fighting off the fierce challenge of French 'team-mate' Michel Rougerie, Villa took the 250 cc title that year and held it for two more seasons. And to cap his career he made it a double in 1976 when he also won the 350 cc title, beating reigning champion Johnny Cecotto.

World Champion: 350 cc 1976.   250 cc 1974, 1975 & 1976

A top ten pop star in his native Japan, Takazumi Katayama was the first and to date the only Japanese rider to win a World Championship – the 350 cc in 1977.

Born in Korea but raised in Kobe, the extrovert Japanese started racing in 1969, winning his national 250 cc title three years later. In 1973 he took the 350 cc Japanese series and this inspired him to try his luck in Europe, with some help from Yamaha for whom he worked as a tester.

He made his début in the 1974 Dutch TT and went on to finish fourth in the 250 cc World Championship, recording his first Grand Prix win in the Swedish event that year.

A hard and forceful rider, 'Zooming Taxi' was involved in some acrimonious post-race enquiries about his tactics in those early days. But he settled down and in 1977 joined the Yamaha team to contest the 350 cc title on a prototype three-cylinder machine. He won the World Championship by a massive margin, but lost it the next year to Kork Ballington and Kawasaki. He also raced a 500 cc Yamaha in 1978, finishing fifth in the championship.

In 1979 he and Mick Grant were teamed on the ill-fated Honda NR500 – the extraordinary four-stroke with which Honda hoped to challenge the two-strokes for Grand Prix honours. When Honda switched to two-strokes, Takazumi stayed with them, winning the 500 cc class of the 1982 Swedish Grand Prix.

Now retired, he lives in France.

SURVIVOR of motor cycle racing's two fastest crashes, Barry Sheene is arguably Britain's most famous two-wheeled star. For despite the fact that he last won the 500 cc title in 1977 he is still a household name. Barry is a genuine 'cockney kid': he was brought up in a basement flat under the Royal College of Surgeons building in Holborn. His father Frank, a racer in pre-war days, was in charge of maintenance there and had his own workshop where he successfully tuned two-strokes ridden by, among others, Phil Read and Bill Ivy.

Obviously it was not long before young Barry was taking a keen interest. Born in 1950, he made his début on one of dad's Spanish-built Bultaco racers at Brands Hatch in 1968. The boy was a natural and in 1970 won his first title, the British 125 cc championship, riding a Bultaco and later an ex-works Suzuki.

In 1971 he went 'continental' for the first time, contesting the 125 cc and 50 cc classes of the classics riding the Suzuki and a works Kreidler. He came close on the bigger machine, finishing runner-up to Angel Nieto, but he got more publicity when he openly criticised the Isle of Man TT. After crashing out of the 125 cc race and retiring from a production machine event there he said he thought the circuit was too dangerous for modern-day racing and that he would never return – a decision he stuck to.

A minor crash cost him any chance of honours in 1972, when he switched to Yamahas, but the following year he joined Suzuki GB, the start of a long and successful partnership. He won the FIM's 750 cc

Sheene in the sunshine. Barry Sheene demonstrates the modern style as he cranks his 500 cc Suzuki around a left-hander during the 1978 Spanish Grand Prix.

championship for them in 1973 and was voted 'Man of the Year' by the readers of *Motor Cycle News*.

In March 1975 came the first horrific accident, at Daytona, when the tread of the rear tyre of his 750 cc Suzuki peeled off and locked the rear wheel at 175 mph. In the ensuing crash Barry suffered a broken thigh, wrist, collarbone and ribs. Yet three months later he won his first 500 cc classic – the Dutch TT!

Sheene won the 500 cc World Championship in 1976, and held it in 1977. But Kenny Roberts (Yamaha) got the better of him the following year, and from then on Barry was up against it.

In 1980 he switched to Yamaha and in 1982, at the British Grand Prix at Silverstone, came the second high-speed crash. It happened during practice when Sheene, flat out, hit a bike that he failed to see lying on the circuit. He suffered appalling injuries to his legs. His fight back to racing fitness was national news and won him a host of new fans. He made it – and less than a year later was racing again, back with Suzuki.

Barry fought hard and in 1984 finished sixth in the 500 cc championship but the Suzuki was no longer competitive and, at the end of the season, he called it a day. After all, he had nothing left to prove.

A charismatic character, Barry was also a schemer. He loved to plot and plan and was for ever on the phone, trying to get more money for this, sponsorship for that, or a better deal for the other. He used to drive Suzuki GB mad – but he was the greatest character the sport has known, and he is now enjoying his retirement in Australia.

NINETEEN-year-old Johnny Cecotto burst onto the European racing scene in 1975 with a run of successes that stunned the established stars and made him a national hero back home in Venezuela.

First he scored a 250/350 cc Yamaha double on his World Championship début at the French Grand Prix in late March. Then, switching to a TZ750 Yamaha, he outlasted an all-star field to win Europe's most prestigious (and most rewarding) big bike race – the Imola 200.

Son of an Italian immigrant, Cecotto started his racing career on a 750 cc Honda when he was 16. The Venezuelan Yamaha importer, Andrea Ippolito, realised his potential and, using his charm and financial clout with the factory, made sure he got the best machines.

Johnny scored his first major success when he came from last to finish third in the Daytona 200 in March 1975. He then made his sensational European Grand Prix début *and* kept up the pressure, to become the youngest rider to have won a World Championship – the 350 cc. It was a record that stood until 1989 when Alex Criville took the 125 cc title.

Following that up he went back to Daytona in 1976 to win there – and at 20 he was the youngest rider ever to win the American classic. He was runner-up in the 350 cc championship that year but a crash early in 1977 put him out of contention for the season.

In 1978 Yamaha moved into the 500 cc class and Cecotto finished third. But Kenny Roberts was now the number one and Cecotto faded from the scene, switching to car racing.

A film star character in Venezuela (I will never forget travelling in his motorcade through the streets of Valencia in 1976, when thousands turned out to cheer him), Cecotto had charisma that came across to the public – just like his great friend, Barry Sheene.

Big bike or small – Johnny Cecotto could ride them all. Here the charismatic Venezuelan gives his 750 cc Yamaha some stick during the 1976 round of the big-bike series in his native country.

FOR just one year the little Italian Morbidelli factory produced a world-beater in the 250 cc class – and Lega was good enough to win the 1977 championship on it. A post office worker from Lugo, he learned his racing on Yamahas.

EUGENIO LAZZARINI

RICARDO TORMO

SMALL and smiling, he graced the paddocks for a number of years before coming good to win the 1978 125 cc World Championship on an MBA and then the 50 cc title on Kreidlers in 1979 and 1980.

COACHED by fellow-Spaniard and Bultaco team-mate Angel Nieto, Tormo responded to win the 50 cc title in 1978 and again in 1981 when he rejoined the Barcelona factory after a spell with Kreidler.

World Champion: 125 cc 1978

World Champion: 50 cc 1979 & 1980

World Champion: 50 cc 1978 & 1981

Y OU never saw George O'Dell without a broad smile on his face. An extrovert character from a working-class Hemel Hempstead background, George appeared perfectly equipped to withstand the ups and downs of life and always to come up smiling.

That appearances can be cruelly deceptive was proved yet again when George took his own life in March 1981. Depressed by his lack of recent racing success and by the break-up of his marriage, the final straw for George came when he heard on the radio that Mike Hailwood had been fatally injured in a road accident.

George came up through the ranks of club racing, riding BSA-powered outfits. He switched to Konig engines and scored his first major success in 1974 when he took second place in the Isle of Man TT – a World Championship round in those days.

Progress was steady and the big break came in 1975 when Eric May, who had a welding business in Windsor, bought George a Yamaha engine. Proving he could use the extra power George set the first-ever 100 mph lap by a sidecar at Silverstone – and two years later he was the first man on three wheels to lap the Isle of Man at over the 'ton'.

Eric helped him to buy an ex-Biland Seymaz chassis for the 1977 season and using that O'Dell, partnered by Kenny Arthur and Cliff Holland, won the world title. But, strange to say, George O'Dell is the only motor cycle World Champion never to have won a Grand Prix.

THE career of Germany's Rolf Steinhausen is the longest of any in top class sidecar racing – 20 years at international level. Yet he only turned to three wheels after two serious accidents, one motor cycling, the second skiing.

Born in 1943 the tall, cheerful German made his racing début on a solo BMW at the Nürburgring when he was 18. He crashed and sustained severe facial injuries. Then, soon after he had recovered, his passion for speed got him into more trouble when a ski hit a hidden rock and broke his left leg so severely that the surgeons had a fight on their hands to save it.

He spent several months in hospital and came out with a left leg thinner and weaker than the right. Most men would have given up any ideas of a road racing career then and there – but not Rolf. He decided to go sidecar racing, starting in 1967 with a BMW.

In 1970 he turned professional, won the German championship and started riding in international events. For the 1972 season he abandoned BMW power and pioneered the use of the Berlin-built, four-cylinder two-stroke Konig engine in sidecar racing.

It was a good move and Rolf battled his way up the ladder. He won his first Grand Prix, the Belgian, in 1974 when he averaged 116.81 mph to beat reigning champion Klaus Enders. And in 1975 he toppled Enders from the head of the table.

Germany's Rolf Steinhausen (Busch-Konig) screws the power on during the 1976 Austrian Grand Prix. His passenger is Jos Huber.

Rolf repeated his success in 1976 and has been among the top ten ever since, abandoning his Dieter Busch-prepared Konig for Yamaha power in recent years, but still easily identifiable as virtually the only top-liner with the sidecar on the right of the machine.

Now, as 1990 looms, Rolf is talking in terms of retiring. Trained as a vehicle mechanic and electrician at the MAN truck plant, he has a wife and two children. When he does quit the sport that he has graced for nearly a quarter of a century, everyone will miss him.

World Champion: Sidecars 1975 & 1976

'ROLF'S worst enemy is the man he sees in the mirror every morning,' said one of Rolf's passengers, when asked to comment on the brilliant Swiss rider's patchy form over his 15 years as a top-flight sidecar racer.

The problem with Rolf is that he is a perfectionist. He is not content to prepare an outfit just to win races – he wants to annihilate the opposition and is always seeking to have the lightest outfit and the fastest engine.

To Biland sidecar racing is a challenge and he is at his happiest when carving chunks off lap records. Often he has cut the margin of safety to the bone, particularly when tuning his Yamaha-based four-cylinder Krauser engines, and has suffered the consequences in mechanical failures.

When it comes to technical innovations no one can match sidecar star Rolf Biland – seen here at the Salzburgring in 1975 on his Yamaha-powered Seymaz.

Rolf knows his weakness, shrugs his shoulders, smiles broadly and keeps on making mistakes. We, the spectators, should be thankful. His natural riding ability is such that if he had had a reliable outfit he could well have won the world title every year since he first finished on top in 1978.

Born and raised in Birmenstorf in German-speaking Switzerland, Rolf was an apprentice in the motor trade when he started racing at the age of 21 in local hill-climbs. In 1974 he went international with a low-slung outfit powered by a three-cylinder Swedish Crescent engine, but for the next season he switched to Yamaha power in a Swiss Seymaz chassis.

From that moment Rolf Biland has always been in the news. At the 1975 Austrian Grand Prix he set the fastest practice lap ahead of three of the then-dominant Konig-engined outfits but retired from the race with engine trouble. The next Sunday he made history when he won the class at the German Grand Prix at Hockenheim – the first victory by a Yamaha-powered outfit.

It was typical of Rolf, partnered in those early days by Freddie Freiburghaus, that he set the fastest practice lap by a clear four seconds and then won the race by the incredible margin of 53 seconds, pushing the lap record up from 95.56 mph to 98.42 mph as he did so. He simply was not content just to win – he went as fast as he could all the way.

His charge for the championship took a knock when the steering of the Seymaz failed, while he was racing flat out in a minor international at Mettet in Belgium. He crashed at 140 mph, missed several races because of injury, but bounced back to finish second at the Dutch TT and take third place in the table at the end of the year.

In 1976 he was plagued by problems, mainly mechanical, and finished fourth. He was runner-up the next year, then won his first World Championship in 1978. He held the title the next year, slipped to second in 1980 before finishing top again in 1981, was runner-up in 1982 and won for the fourth time in 1983.

It was too easy in a way. Rolf was getting bored and went off occasionally to race cars. He still placed regularly, though, and came back with a bang in 1988, stimulated by the new challenge posed by the Steve Webster/Tony Hewitt duo. The championship went right to the last round. Biland only had to finish in the points in Czechoslovakia to regain his crown – but gearbox failure cost him the title.

Rolf challenged strongly in 1989 but again the occasional retirement let him down. It doesn't really worry Rolf, though. He loves to race – and he loves to experiment. He simply cannot resist a challenge.

World Champion: Sidecars 1978, 1979, 1981 & 1983

AMERICAN rivals dubbed him Kenny Robot and the name was apt. For the little Californian lacked the charm and sparkle of the first wave of American racers – men like Dick Mann, Gary Nixon and Gene Romero.

Kenny went about his business in a deadly serious and totally dedicated way. And no one can deny that, for him, it worked, for he was the first American to win a World Championship – the 500 cc in 1978. He repeated the feat in 1979, and again in 1980. Then came two hard years when injury and machines that were not quite as good as the opposition put him out of contention before he and Yamaha waged a titanic battle with Freddie Spencer and Honda for the 500 cc crown in 1983.

It went to the penultimate round in Sweden – where Freddie outfought Kenny. The will to win of the younger man was irresistible. True, he virtually pushed Roberts off the circuit on the final lap, but the important thing was that Spencer won the race and the championship.

Although still only in his early 30s Kenny had been racing virtually non-stop ever since he was 14. He was astute enough to know that it was time to quit. He raced a few more times, then switched to managing the Lucky Strike Yamaha team.

His career started, as did that of so many Americans, on the local dirt-tracks, where he learned to control a wheel-spinning, sliding machine. Those lessons stood him in good stead throughout his career.

He won the American Motorcyclist Association Novice championship in 1970, was Junior champion the following year, and in 1973 and again in 1974 was the AMA Grand National champion – and to win that title in those days you had to be a star at both road racing and dirt-track. All these successes were achieved on Yamahas.

In 1974 he made a brief visit to Europe, to race a 250 cc in the Dutch TT. He challenged Walter Villa early on, eventually finishing third.

In the USA he concentrated more and more on road racing. Finally, in 1978, Yamaha decided to back him in their effort to wrest the 500 cc world title from Suzuki and Barry Sheene. Roberts succeeded brilliantly, despite the fact that he had to learn a new circuit at every Grand Prix. He clinched the title at the British Grand Prix at Silverstone, in a race unfortunately ruined by rain.

His successes during the following two seasons were far more decisive. And it was during this period that he tried to launch the World Series, a breakaway 250 cc and 500 cc championship outside the jurisdiction of the FIM, the sport's governing body. The bid failed and Kenny was a bitter man.

Armco alley! American eagle Kenny Roberts (Yamaha) cuts close to the steel barrier during the 1978 Belgian Grand Prix.

World Champion: 500 cc 1978, 1979 & 1980

IT was Scruffy Gibson who first told me about Kork Ballington, in the late Sixties. 'There's a youngster out here who's going to be really good. He could make it right to the top,' wrote Scruffy, a newspaper reporter in Pietermaritzburg, South Africa, and correspondent for *Motor Cycle*.

He was right. Hugh Neville Ballington, Korky or Kork from his schooldays, more than fulfilled Scruffy's prophecy. Racing first Yamahas and then Kawasakis, he won a total of 31 Grands Prix and four World Championships – figures which put him firmly among the sport's top 20 riders.

Small, quiet and determined, Kork started racing in 1967 when he was 16 on the Roy Hesketh circuit on the outskirts of Pietermaritzburg. Riding a variety of machines he was soon winning races and championships in South Africa.

Ever since he had read, as a schoolboy, of the exploits of fellow-South African Paddy Driver and of Rhodesian-based Gary Hocking and Jim Redman, Kork's ambition had been to race in the World Championships. His chance came when he won a 'Rider to Europe' sponsorship award at a South African meeting.

It was an uphill struggle, but he eventually broke through in 1976. In August that year he finished second in the 250 cc class of the West German Grand Prix at the famous

South African Kork Ballington aboard his 250 cc Kawasaki during the 1978 Venezuelan Grand Prix. He won four championships for the Japanese factory.

Nürburgring – and in September he won his first World Championship race, the 350 cc class of the Spanish Grand Prix at the wonderful old Montjuich Park circuit overlooking Barcelona.

Realising the potential of the little South African, Midlands sponsor Syd Griffiths equipped him with a pair of new Yamahas for 1977. Kork, with brother Dozey as chief mechanic, responded by scoring his first 250/350 cc double at the British Grand Prix at Silverstone, and by placing sixth and fourth in the respective championships.

In 1978 Kawasaki came into road racing with a bang. Signing Mick Grant, Australian Gregg Hansford and Ballington they set out to win both the 250 cc and 350 cc titles with their neat little water-cooled, two-stroke 'tandem' twins – one cylinder behind the other rather than side by side.

Of the three, Ballington was the underdog but matching riding ability with tactics it was Kork who triumphed. In the bigger class he beat Yamaha's Takazumi Katayama by the massive margin of 57 points and in the smaller he got the better of Hansford in a far tougher struggle.

Kork repeated the double dose in 1979. In 1980 he was runner-up in the 250 cc class but, by then, he was more interested in Kawasaki's 500 cc challenge. Riding the big four-cylinder he put in some fine performances but was never quite able to match the best in the class.

After racing the big Kawasaki for three years Kork quit the European scene. His career took on a new lease of life when he raced a Honda in the American 250 cc championship, winning the Daytona 100 in 1987 and taking second place in the overall championship. A slide down to tenth place the following year persuaded him it was time to pack it in.

World Champion: 350 cc 1978 & 1979.   250 cc 1978 & 1979

PAOLO PILERI

PIER-PAOLO BIANCHI

S WARTHY Italian born in 1944 who dominated the 125 cc championship in 1975, winning seven of the ten Grands Prix on a factory twin-cylinder Morbidelli.

A mechanic by trade and with a build ideally suited to the smaller machines, he combined his early racing with working at the Morbidelli factory near his home town of Rimini. Won the 1976 and 1977 World Championships for Morbidelli and the 1980 title for MBA.

World Champion: 125 cc 1975

World Champion: 125 cc 1976, 1977 & 1980

Ginger Molloy: high-spirited New Zealander who was a member of the continental circus for many years. Rode works Bultacos, finishing third in the 125 cc series in 1968, but had his most successful season in 1970 when he raced a Kawasaki to second place in the 500 cc table.

Keith Turner: hard-riding New Zealander who raced a Suzuki twin to runner-up spot in the 500 cc table in 1971, scoring second places in Austria, East Germany and Sweden.

Rob Bron: cheerful Dutchman who made the most of getting one of the first batch of twin-cylinder Suzuki racers, to finish third in the 1971 500 cc championship.

Angelo Bergamonti: made his name racing Paton and
Aermacchi machines in the 500 cc class and was so
successful on the latter in 1970, finishing third in the
World Championship, that he was signed by MV
Agusta. He won the Spanish Grand Prix for MV
Agusta late that year but tragically, having made the
breakthrough, was fatally injured when he crashed in
a rain-swept meeting at Riccione in April 1971.

Left: Alberto Pagani: like his World Championship-winning father, Alberto was quiet, well spoken and thoughtful. He was recruited into the MV Agusta team after the death of Bergamonti and was runner-up to team-mate Agostini in the 1972 500 cc championship.

Below: Kim Newcombe: big, blond New Zealander who built and raced a 500 cc powered by a flat-four Konig engine in the 1973 championship. When Yamaha withdrew, following the death of Saarinen, Kim took on the MV Agustas. He lost his life in an accident at Silverstone, but still finished second in the table.

Gianfranco Bonera: gained experience racing a 750 cc Triumph in long-distance events before making his name internationally on the two-stroke Italian-built Harley-Davidsons. Left them to join MV Agusta, where he replaced Agostini and teamed with Phil Read, taking second place behind Read in the 1974 500 cc table.

THE GRAND PRIX RIDERS

Chas Mortimer: son of a pre-war Brooklands star, Chas was the Americans' idea of an English sportsman, extrovert and well spoken. Raced just about everything, but had his greatest successes on 125 cc Yamahas in 1972 and 1973 when he finished third and then second in the championship. Kept going to take third place in the 350 cc table in 1976, again Yamaha mounted.

Tom Herron: dark, friendly Irishman who, Yamaha mounted, battled his way to second place in the 1977 350 cc championship. Lost his life in an accident at the North West 200 in May 1979.

John Dodds: yet another good Australian rider who made his name racing Nortons before switching to Yamahas. Won the FIM 750 cc championship in 1974 and finished third in the 250 cc World Championship in 1973. Now lives in Germany.

Above: Hideo Kanaya: the first Japanese rider to win a 500 cc World Championship race. He achieved this riding a works Yamaha at the ultra-fast Austrian Grand Prix in 1975, and went on to finish third in the table.

Left: Bruno Kneubühler: chirpy little Swiss who first made his mark by finishing third on a Yamaha in the 500 cc series in 1972. Has raced in every solo class since then, taking second in the 50 cc table on a Kreidler the next year, then second in the 125 cc on a Yamaha in 1974. Incredibly kept going and raced a Honda in the 1989 500 cc series!

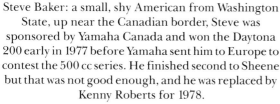

Steve Baker: a small, shy American from Washington State, up near the Canadian border, Steve was sponsored by Yamaha Canada and won the Daytona 200 early in 1977 before Yamaha sent him to Europe to contest the 500 cc series. He finished second to Sheene but that was not good enough, and he was replaced by Kenny Roberts for 1978.

Tepi Lansivuori: an undertaker from the far north of Finland, Tepi was badly hit by the death of his friend and hero Jarno Saarinen. But he soldiered on to finish second in both the 250 cc and 350 cc championships in 1973, and was third in the 500 cc table the following year – all on Yamahas. He then switched to Suzuki and was runner-up to Barry Sheene in the 1976 500 cc series.

Michel Rougerie: dark and sallow, Michel looked a bit of a villain – and there was certainly strong rivalry between him and Harley-Davidson team-mate, Walter Villa, when Villa won the 250 cc title in 1975 with Michel second. Left Harley to race Yamahas with Elf sponsorship, but was killed in an accident at the Salzburgring in 1981.

Patrick Fernandez: dashingly dark, a typical son of the Provençal region of France, Patrick came from St Tropez. Finished third in the 250 cc championship in 1978 and second in the 350 cc the next year when, on his private Yamaha, he split the works Kawasakis.

Patrick Pons: first Frenchman really to make it to the top, Patrick was a quiet, studious character who starred on Sonauto-sponsored Yamahas. He won the FIM 750 cc championship in 1979, placed in many Grands Prix, won the Daytona 200 early in 1981 but died in a racing accident later that year.

Pat Hennen: gutsy Californian who starred for Suzuki
with third places in the 500 cc table in 1976 and 1977,
only to have his career cut short when he suffered
severe head injuries after crashing in the Isle of Man
in June 1978.

Gregg Hansford: big, blond beach-boy Australian who
came to Europe with a reputation he never quite lived
up to. Had two good years with the Kawasaki team,
though, twice finishing second in the 250 cc
championship and twice taking third place in
the 350 cc.

Wil Hartog: tall, good-looking Dutch farmer who was always immaculately turned out in white leathers and red, white and blue helmet. Achieved his life's ambition in 1977 when, Suzuki mounted, he won the 500 cc class of the Dutch TT before a crowd of 140,000 partisan fans. He went on to win four more 500 cc Grands Prix.

Virginio Ferrari: shot to brief fame in 1979 when he led the Suzuki challenge and finished second to Kenny Roberts in the 500 cc championship.

THE EIGHTIES

Knee-pad skimming the track, rear wheel sliding under power, yet Eddie Lawson looks completely at ease as he heads for the 1988 500 cc title on his Yamaha.

By PETER CLIFFORD

ANTON MANG

YOUNG riders are often aggressive, but it's a characteristic that usually becomes tempered with age and experience. Germany's Anton Mang maintained his aggression all the way through his final championship-winning season in 1987. It was his third 250 cc title: he had won the same championship in 1980 and '81, and the 350 cc in 1981 and '82.

It might be argued that those early championship wins were easier for Mang because he had the use of the best equipment in the class, the factory Kawasakis. And he was unable to demonstrate that he was superior to previous winner Kork Ballington, because he took over the titles as the South African moved to the 500 class. But there is no doubt that Toni improved as he gained more experience. By 1987 he was both the fastest and the most experienced 250 rider in the world – and there were plenty of other factory machines by then to provide strong opposition.

Mang learnt that essential aggression from some hard teachers. When he raced against Ballington he was up against one of the most skilled World Champions ever, but when he lost the 350 cc title to Jon Ekerold in 1980 he was beaten by a man whose bywords were determination and aggression. Before their final clash of the season at the classic Nürburgring Ekerold said, 'It is either win or crash for me.'

Mang was meant to hear those words – and he could not cope with that sort of attitude at that point in his career. He never became a crash-or-win rider, but in his later seasons there was no one harder and some of the top 250 cc men felt intimidated when racing against him. He could win on any circuit, against any opposition, very often leading from the front and just increasing the pace gradually until the pack behind cracked.

Bavarian Toni Mang, winner of more 250 cc Grands Prix than any other rider, in typical pose on his factory Honda during the 1987 Spanish Grand Prix.

His 42nd and final Grand Prix win was typical. It was the Japanese Grand Prix at the beginning of 1988 and Toni had to fight off local hero Masahiro Kobayashi, who had won the race the previous year, John Kocinski, the Grand Prix newcomer hot for instant stardom, and Sito Pons, who went on to win the World Championship. At times it was a six-man fight for the lead but Mang put in a perfect final lap and just pulled out enough of a gap to prevent a last-corner effort from Pons.

Mang might have gone on to retain his title, in what he intended should be his last season, but a high-speed fall in the third round at Járama made him think a little more about retiring with a healthy body. After two third-place finishes in the middle of the season he had a first-corner mid-pack collision in Yugoslavia and broke his collarbone. He decided not to return to racing when it healed and let two of Germany's up and coming riders, Jochen Schmid and Helmut Bradl, use the machines at the end of the season.

Toni had plans to run a team in 1990 but could not organise the necessary sponsorship. He remained determined to have his own team in the near future.

THE last of the truly flamboyant Italian World Champions, Marco won his single 500 cc World Championship on Roberto Gallina's Suzuki in 1981. Born in 1954, he only began racing when he was nearly 20 but made incredibly rapid progress. He rode in his first Grand Prix the next season, finishing seventh at Imola, his favourite circuit.

Lucchinelli's championship fortunes varied as he changed teams and machines – and spent too much time enjoying life. His fourth place in 1976 was impressive for a newcomer to the 500 cc class, but he only scored in four of the ten rounds after missing several races thanks to two crashes. He had the backing then of Gallina, himself a successful racer, but left Gallina's team at the end of the season. The move proved disastrous.

It was only when Marco returned to the same fold in 1980 that he again had an impact on the results. He finished third in the championship, even though the bike was not perfectly reliable. The bike could have been better but it was the team which seemed to exert enough of an influence over Lucchinelli to channel his energies in the right direction. The following year the bike did not stop and Marco won the World Championship.

He then sold his services to the highest bidder, Honda. An unlucky fall early in the season, which resulted in an injured ankle, ruined any chance of him carrying on where he had left off with Suzuki and he never regained his form or his concentration.

In 1988 he took part in the less demanding World Superbike Championship and, riding for Ducati, finished fifth.

World Champion: 500 cc 1981

A true professional who did a great deal to help the sport develop in the early Eighties as a spokesman respected by all, his near-fatal accident at Assen in 1983 challenged his strength of character as much as winning the 500 cc World Championship had done the previous season. Uncini fought back to full health and raced again in 1984, finishing fifth in the second Grand Prix of the year near his home at Misano. But the rest of his season was not as impressive, the Suzuki was no longer competitive and Franco had lost the need to win. Not surprisingly, the accident had made him view life a little differently.

Born in 1955, he started racing in 1974 and by 1976 was competing in the World Championships. He finished second to Mario Lega in the 1977 250 cc championship riding a factory Harley-Davidson two-stroke twin.

When he switched to the 500 cc class in '79 it was as a privateer. He was an impressive fifth that season and did one better the next year. In 1981 he was simply unbelievably unlucky with unreliable machinery – so when Marco Lucchinelli won the championship and left Roberto Gallina's factory Suzuki team, Uncini was a natural replacement.

On the right machine at last Franco was simply unbeatable in '82. He took the title with three of the twelve races still to go, and had won five of the eight races that the top men contested. (Uncini was at the centre of the boycott of the French round at Nogaro, where the top riders decided that the circuit was simply not up to standard.)

The Nogaro boycott was just one of the instances when Uncini's command of languages and highly respected professionalism helped unite the riders in a well-reasoned cause. At other times Franco's ability to talk equally well with the FIM avoided ultimate confrontation.

World Champion: 500 cc 1982

WHEN Jock Taylor and Benga Johansson won the Sidecar World
Championship in 1980 it marked a resurgence of power in the class for
Britain. Although George O'Dell had won the title in 1977 he did not
make the same impact as Taylor, who was universally respected as one of the very
best sidecar drivers.

Not only was Taylor respected, he was also very well liked and a tremendous
ambassador for the sport. The Scot had the happy knack of talking easily to
anyone and he did a great deal for sidecar racing, especially in Britain.

Born in 1954, his first racing ambition was to do well at the Isle of Man TT. He
won there for the first time in 1978, and again in '80 and '81. He loved the TT and
did not find the danger unacceptable. Indeed, the level of risk he was prepared to
accept would be quite out of step with the thinking of today's champions. Jock
wanted to race at Imatra in 1982, even though conditions were terrible and the risk
of a sidecar aquaplaning on the slippery public roads was high. He lost control of
his outfit at high speed and later died of his injuries.

Rolf Biland had argued before the race that they should not start, but he could
not get enough support from the other competitors. After the event Rolf was
desolated and said that no sport was worth the loss of life. It is unlikely that Jock
Taylor would have seen it like that.

BEING brought up in Assen it was natural that Streuer would be interested in racing – but not every local goes as far as taking part and no one has been so successful. Born in 1954, Egbert started racing in 1975 but it was not until 1980 that he made an all-out attack on the World Championship, when he finished fourth. Fast and consistent, he only failed to score once, in Finland, when he and passenger Johan van der Kaap crashed.

Streuer developed not only as a rider but also as a tuner. By 1983 he and his machinery were fast enough to take second in the title race and he had teamed with Bernard Schnieders. The two made a contrasting pair, Streuer thin with a wildly bushy beard and muscular Schnieders with chiselled features and blue eyes that sent the girls wild. The combination was good enough to give them three straight World Championship wins, in 1984, '85 and '86. They were popular victors and Streuer was always willing to help out fellow-racers with advice and parts – a typical sidecar competitor.

Streuer continued his engineering experiments and made his own extensive modifications to the old 500 Yamaha engines, rather than adopting the Krauser engines that became so popular with almost all the other teams. His experimentation may have generated a little unreliability but he has remained a top competitor and frequent Grand Prix winner.

World Champion: Sidecars 1984, 1985 & 1986

JON EKEROLD

JEAN-LOUIS TOURNADRE

UNIVERSALLY recognised as one of the 'hard men' of Grand Prix racing. Winning the 350 cc title in 1980, he was one of the last true privateer World Champions and had to fight for that privilege against Toni Mang on the ex-works Kawasaki.

Born in Johannesburg in 1950, Jon started racing in 1969 and made a stunning Grand Prix début at the Salzburgring in 1975, finishing second in the 350 cc race. Never an ally of authority, the tall South African was greatly skilled but won on determination as much as anything.

A quiet, serious rider who kept very much to himself, he was accompanied to races by his father, who helped as mechanic, and won the 250 cc World Championship in 1982.

Born in Clermont-Ferrand in 1958 he started racing in 1977 and only made his Grand Prix début in 1980. He had won the French 750 championship the previous year. In 1982 he won the French Grand Prix – boycotted by Toni Mang, who was to lose the championship by a single point – and claimed the title with consistent placings in the other rounds.

World Champion: 350 cc 1980

World Champion: 250 cc 1982

STEFAN DÖRFLINGER

BY being both the last World Champion of the old 50 cc formula and the first on an 80 cc bike, the Swiss secured a special place in history. A run of four World Championships between 1982 and 1985 was achieved with a combination of skill and experience, for he had been racing since 1970.

He was born in Nagold, Germany in 1948 and made his Grand Prix début at the Hockenheimring in 1973, finishing eleventh on a Kreidler. Though he almost always campaigned a 125 as well as the smaller single, he was never as successful on the bigger machine.

World Champion: 80 cc 1984 & 1985.   50 cc 1982 & 1983

WERNER SCHWÄRZEL

CONSISTENCY won the German pair of Schwärzel and Andreas Huber the Sidecar World Championship in 1982, for although they did not win a Grand Prix they finished every race and were on the rostrum in seven of the nine races. Rolf Biland and Kurt Waltisperg did most of the winning, but they failed to score three times.

Schwärzel was born in Meissenheim in 1948 and started racing in 1970. He won ten Grands Prix in his career and dominated the German sidecar championship from 1974 until he retired at the end of the 1985 season.

World Champion: Sidecars 1982

125

THE way in which Freddie Spencer dominated both the 250 cc and 500 cc World Championships in 1985 ensured him a place in any racing history – and he had already won the 500 cc title in 1983, after a year-long, fierce struggle with Kenny Roberts. Spencer had an incredible talent and it seemed a good bet that he would dominate the sport for the best part of the Eighties.

Incredibly, he never won another Grand Prix. Far from being the most successful rider of the second half of the decade he became the most disappointing, with a series of mysterious injuries, non-appearances and unSpencer-like performances. He has always remained a very private person, so we may never know what went wrong. A professional who gave good interviews with lengthy explanations, he nevertheless had an unsurpassed ability to avoid the crux of a question if he wished to.

It is unrewarding to dwell on what went wrong, much more enjoyable to recall the great years – and there were many of those, for Freddie started racing dirt-track at the age of six. Born on 20 December 1961, by 1976 he had established himself as a road racer and was the West and Eastern Racing Association Racer of the Year. By the time he was 16 he had won every race in the American Motorcyclist Association national novice division championship.

Spencer made his Grand Prix début at Zolder in 1980 but retired early with mechanical problems. He then rode the ill-fated NR500 Honda four-stroke at Silverstone in the British Grand Prix the following season, pushing it harder than anyone else who was unlucky enough to be part of the project. It was no fault of his that the bike broke.

Let it all hang out! Freddie Spencer demonstrates the modern Cossack style as he powers his four-cylinder Honda to victory in the 1985 Italian Grand Prix.

Honda produced the NS500 three-cylinder two-stroke for 1982 so that they could expunge the disappointment of the NR. Spencer won his first Grand Prix with it that season at Spa in Belgium. He was all set for a serious attack on the World Championship in '83.

Those Roberts–Spencer battles of 1983 were classic contests. They had six wins each and six pole positions apiece in the 12-race series, and there have been few more exciting struggles. Spencer won the first three races, then Roberts fought back strongly. In the end, Freddie took the title by just two points. Who can say where the championship was won and lost? But at the second-to-last round at Anderstorp in Sweden the final lap was certainly pivotal – and memorable.

With just two corners to go, Spencer and Roberts were braking side by side at the end of the back straight. Spencer, on the inside, let the brakes off and got into the corner slightly ahead but going a little too fast. Both men ran onto the dirt on the way out – but Spencer was first back on the track, and first across the line. 'I underestimated what he was prepared to do to win,' said Roberts later.

World Champion: 500 cc 1983 & 1985.   250 cc 1985

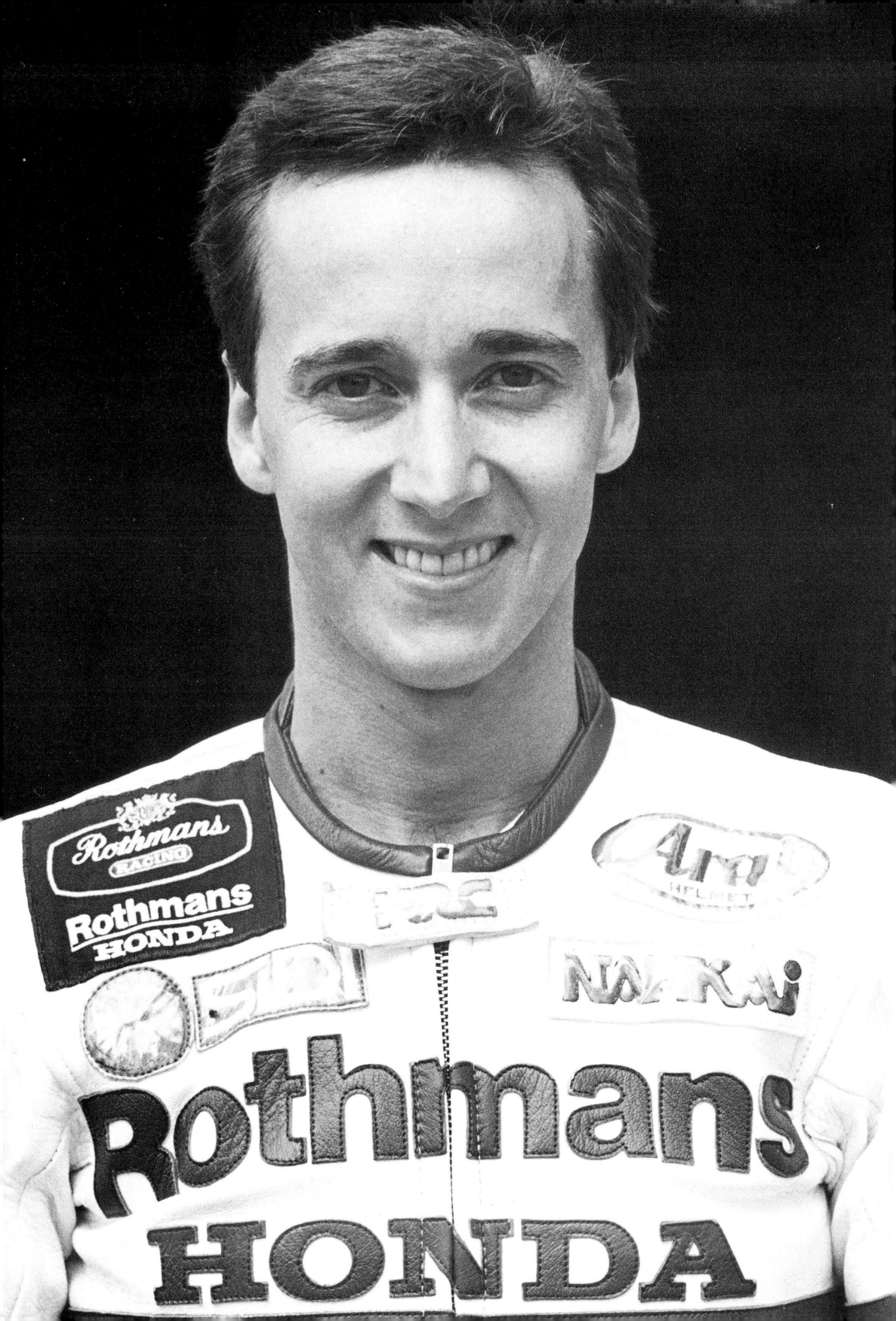
Rothmans
RACING
Rothmans
HONDA
Rothmans
HONDA

WELL loved for his cheeky humour, fast but a little accident prone, the Frenchman acquired the nickname 'Tarzan' because of his weedy appearance. In the late Eighties he was the only European to offer any sort of challenge to the American domination of the 500 cc class and was at least a regular on the rostrum, even if he missed out on the Grand Prix wins.

Born in 1955 and a graduate of the Kawasaki Cup in France, Sarron had his initial success and won his single World Championship on the smaller 250 cc machines – but he always said he preferred 500s and 750s.

He shot to prominence in 1977 when he won the thrilling 250 cc German Grand Prix at the Hockenheimring on a Yamaha, beating the factory Kawasaki of Akihiro Kiyohara. Christian only scored on one other occasion that season on the 250 but was second in the Formula 750 series. It was his third racing season.

1978 saw Sarron third on the 750, but his Grand Prix success did not match that on the bigger machine. Thinking that he would therefore do better on a 500 he rode that class as well as the 750 in '79 but failed to shine – and fell too often.

Both 1980 and '81 were pretty disastrous, so it was back to the 250 for 1982. He finished tenth in the championship but in '83 he was second: obviously his skill had finally matured to the point where he was a world title-winning possibility. And in 1984 he put together an impressive series of rostrum positions on a Sonauto Yamaha that secured him the 250 cc World Championship.

Back on the 500 since then he has still hurt himself more often than is prudent, but he has also had a string of good championship positions, finishing third in '85, when he won the wet German Grand Prix, and in 1989 when he was the only other rider to score as consistently as Lawson.

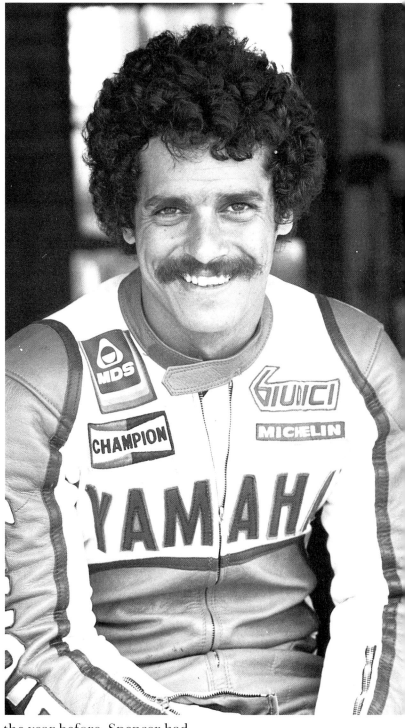

ONE of the most dramatic men to watch on a 250, the Venezuelan earnt a reputation as a crasher right from the start of his Grand Prix career. Born in 1956 in Caracas he started racing in 1976 and had his Grand Prix chance when the World Championships came to Venezuela in 1978.

Carlos caused a minor sensation by finishing second to Kenny Roberts and ahead of much more experienced men on better machinery, but it was viewed as a 'flash in the pan' result from a local hero. And when he followed the rest of the riders to Europe his appalling crash rate seemed to confirm that.

Lavado stuck to it, though, and riding both 250 cc and 350 cc Yamahas for Venemotos, the enthusiastic South American importer, he gradually improved, finishing sixth in the 250 cc class in 1980, fourth in '81 and fifth in '82.

In 1983 he won the 250 cc World Championship by riding as fast as ever and avoiding the mistakes. He had calmed down on the track, but off the bike he was still the crazy, cheerful character who had become so popular in the paddock. Most Grand Prix regulars pick up a reasonable amount of English, out of necessity. Carlos never has. He communicates with his hands, a few words of some language or other, and a broad grin.

He won the championship again in 1986, when Yamaha finally produced a full factory bike to compete with the V-twin that Honda had given Freddie Spencer the year before. Spencer had said, while winning the championship in '85, that Lavado was the one rider he feared, the one who never gave up.

That second championship-winning year he was still capable of overstepping the mark. In Yugoslavia he was last off the line, by lap 11 he was leading and pulling away, the next lap he crashed. Down in 26th place he set off again to catch up and was gaining on the leaders at over a second a lap when his team told him to pull in as he could not regain the lead!

T HE best thing that Eddie Lawson ever did was to leave the Marlboro Yamaha Team at the end of the 1988 season, after winning his third World Championship for them. Not that the team he had been with since his 500 cc Grand Prix début in 1983 were uncompetitive, quite the opposite – the move made Lawson draw more from himself than he had in all the previous six years of his Grand Prix career.

His fourth World Championship, on the Rothmans Honda, elevated him in terms of the respect demanded by his achievement. The Honda was not a good machine to ride and Lawson had a great deal of trouble with it, especially early in the season. He and engineer Erv Kanemoto did what they could to improve it but, in the end, it was down to Eddie to ride harder.

Ice-cool Eddie Lawson in action on his works 500 cc Yamaha in Spain in 1986. Eddie proved himself the top man of the Eighties by winning the 500 cc crown four times.

He responded magnificently and, as he fought the wayward machine, eradicated his old nickname 'Steady Eddie'. His fourth world title, against strong opposition from Wayne Rainey and Kevin Schwantz, meant his supporters could claim for him the title of 'greatest rider of the decade'.

His detractors had always maintained that the championships he won in 1984 and '86 were gifted to him because his arch-rival Freddie Spencer was not fit. As Lawson pointed out, the idea of racing is not to fall off and to stay clear of injury. Even his third championship was won on a Yamaha that was clearly superior to the Honda ridden by Wayne Gardner. It was only when he changed to Honda and won that he finally silenced all the disparaging voices.

Winning four World Championships did not make Eddie popular with everyone. His singleminded determination to succeed on the track apparently left him with little energy for courting favour off the machine. He considered that his job was to be the fastest rider on the track, while relationships with the press, sponsors or other riders in the paddock were an irrelevance that he could do without.

At home in California, away from racing, Lawson remained very much a motor cyclist any enthusiast could identify with, at least in his dreams. With enough money to have any machine he wished for, his huge garage has always housed a large collection of road and dirt bikes, used almost daily. On the road Lawson respects the dangers as greater than on a race track. On the dirt he has always been extremely talented, a fine motocross rider as well as an excellent dirt-tracker – which is where he started his competition career. He rides motocross because he enjoys it, not just for training – but it is his ability to ride any machine, in any conditions, that has made him so successful.

World Champion: 500 cc 1984, 1986, 1988 & 1989

THERE are occasions when a sportsman's personal struggle and achievement so catch the imagination of his country that he becomes a national celebrity. Not only did Wayne Gardner do that when he won the 500 cc World Championship in 1987, but his triumph forced Grand Prix racing to the front of Australia's consciousness.

Gardner worked as hard at promoting himself and the sport as he did at racing – and he fitted the role of Australian underdog who took on the world and won. His riding style was so dramatic that he was obviously trying at every corner, with the bike sliding wildly and threatening to throw him off almost every lap. The fact that he stayed on seemed miraculous at times. Wayne usually avoided crashing out of races, but he did occasionally fall in practice and the way he continued to race with painful injuries added to the heroic image.

Gardner's Grand Prix career started with a half-season in 1984. In 1985 he was fourth on the three-cylinder Honda while the best of the opposition had four-cylinder machines. In '86 Wayne was handed the mantle of team-leader when Honda's number one, Freddie Spencer, pulled out of the first race. Eddie Lawson won the title but Gardner learnt all the way and was obviously going to be an even greater threat to Lawson in 1987.

It was a great year of head-to-head battles between the two men, with Randy Mamola adding another dimension to the contest. The sight of Gardner fighting the Honda at every turn so contrasted with Lawson's cool, subdued, accurate guidance of the Yamaha that the Australian gained a great many fans. He clinched the championship by dominating the Brazilian Grand Prix, and that typified the way he had attacked the season.

Balancing act. Wayne Gardner drifts his factory 500 cc Honda during the 1988 Japanese Grand Prix. The previous year the gutsy Aussie had broken the American domination of the class to win the championship.

Winning the World Championship did not take the edge off his aggression in 1988, but that essential element, luck, totally deserted him. The Honda broke down twice when Wayne might have won races – and the bike handled in an even more wicked manner than it had the previous year. No matter how desperate the situation, though, Gardner never gave up. And that gained him even more respect.

The pressure of racing Lawson for every point intensified for the 1989 season, when the Californian joined the Rothmans Honda team. Gardner later accused Honda of being utterly insensitive to his situation and said that he became preoccupied by thoughts of racing his team-mate.

Wayne did win the most intense race of the season, the first-ever Australian Grand Prix, after an epic battle with Wayne Rainey, Christian Sarron and Kevin Magee. It confirmed his position as a superstar in Australia – but a week later he crashed heavily in America, trying to beat Lawson, and broke his leg badly. Not only did that wreck his season, but Gardner admitted that it had forced him to think long and hard about his own fallibility.

There was no doubt that Gardner still had the talent to be a World Champion. It was now a question of self-confidence – and Wayne knew that any chance of getting back to his best form in 1990 depended on recapturing that confidence.

World Champion: 500 cc 1987

SPAIN dominated the smaller classes throughout the 1970s, thanks to Angel Nieto, but although Ricardo Tormo seemed to offer the possibility of a successor, when he won the 50 cc title for a second time in 1981, he was forced into retirement after a nasty accident testing a racing bike on the road.

The strength in depth of talent was bound to produce a successor before long, and it was Jorge Martinez who was the next Spanish World Champion when he won the first of his 80 cc titles in 1986, ending the four-year reign of Swiss Stefan Dörflinger who had covered the change from 50 cc to 80 cc.

Born in 1962, 'Aspar' is still based in Alzira, Valencia. He started racing in 1979 and made his Grand Prix début in 1982 at Járama on a 50 cc Bultaco, finishing eleventh in the championship. He had already won his first Spanish 50 cc title the previous season – and he took six straight Spanish championships!

In 1984 he joined Derbi but did not star in the early part of the season: he had a string of poor starts, and the Derbi was prone to slow with a misfire or other problems even though it finished races.

Second in the 80 cc championship in 1985, he went on to win in 1986, '87 and '88. In 1988 he became double World Champion by gaining the 125 cc title as well: Garelli's domination of that championship was ended when the rules changed the class from twin- to single-cylinder engines. Aspar totally dominated both classes, only being beaten once in each and crashing once from the 125 in the pouring rain in Germany, after getting on the bigger Derbi straight from winning on the 80 cc bike, and probably too wet and cold to concentrate properly.

But 1989 was to be a disaster for Aspar. A string of mechanical failures hit the Derbi team and, trying to make up for them, Martinez crashed a few times. He finished ninth on the 125 and eighth in the last-ever 80 cc World Championship.

World Champion: 125 cc 1988.   80 cc 1986, 1987 & 1988

LUCA CADALORA

FAUSTO GRESINI

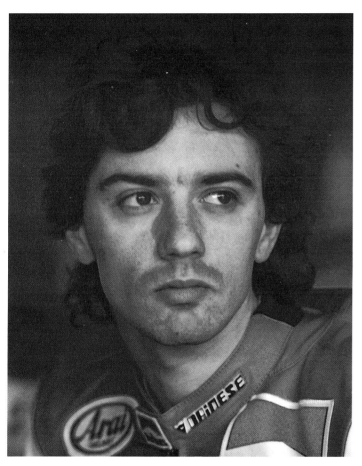

FEW riders have been able to ride a 250 more obviously on the limit and, on occasions, his passing manoeuvres need to be seen to be believed. Off the track Luca is a quiet, reflective character; born in Modena in 1963, he started racing in 1979. His big break came when he joined the Garelli team, for whom he won the 125 cc World Championship in 1986. Giacomo Agostini then signed him to ride 250 Yamahas in his team. He finished second three times that year, in 1988 he won both the German and British Grands Prix, and in '89 he finished fifth in the World Championship, again with two wins.

WHEN he won his second 125 cc World Championship in 1987 he was the number one rider for Garelli and had the best machine in the class. It was the sixth straight championship win for the team and Gresini had already won the title for them in '85. In 1986, though, he finished second after a season-long battle with his team-mate, Luca Cadalora, who refused to take heed of the fact that there were supposed to be team orders. The 125 cc class changed to single-cylinder engines for 1988, however, and the new Garelli was not competitive.

World Champion: 125 cc 1986

World Champion: 125 cc 1985 & 1987

THERE are few racers who have made such complete World Champions. The Spaniard not only proved himself convincingly the best 250 cc racer of 1988 and '89 but he also presented himself extremely well, needing no PR backing at all, did his own sponsorship negotiations *and* created his own team. He still found time to be riders' representative and, during the off-season, when he was not organising or training, to work in his father's business as an architect!

Pons started racing in 1979, in one of Spain's popular one-make cups, and towards the end of that year had his

Spaniard Sito Pons at work on his 250 cc Honda in 1987. He finished third in the championship that year but won the title in 1988 and retained it in 1989.

first test on the Rotax-engined 250 Siroko. He was second in the Spanish championship on that machine the following season and then attacked the World Championship in 1981, gaining a seventh place in the Belgian Grand Prix.

He progressed in 1983, but too often made mistakes, twice while battling for the lead in France and Italy, and then crashed heavily in Austria when Donnie Robinson fell in front of him. That ruined his season. The following year saw his first Grand Prix win, still on a Rotax-engined machine but now called a Kobas with a frame built by Antonio Cobas. The Spanish engineer has played an important part in much of Pons's career.

1985 might be deemed a mistake for Pons as he swapped to the 500 cc class, riding an HB Suzuki alongside Franco Uncini as part of Roberto Gallina's team. He finished equal twelfth in the World Championship on a bike that was not really competitive, as Suzuki had stopped development. But in joining Gallina's team Sito had made another important decision – and that was to give up his studies as an architect to concentrate on racing. Having made the choice he did not back out after that frustrating season. Instead, with a huge budget behind him from Campsa, the Spanish national petrol company, he set up his own team to attack the 250 cc World Championship; he was also fortunate to receive factory backing from Honda.

Pons won the Yugoslav and Belgian Grands Prix and finished second in the championship with a very consistent season. It seemed that his slightly accident-prone reputation had been unjust. But falls haunted him again in 1987 and, although he only fell twice, he was injured both times. He bounced back to win the last race of the year and took third in the title chase.

He finally eradicated all misfortune in 1988. With Cobas helping him make the factory Honda better than the other six factory machines, Pons proved to be both fast and consistent. He won the World Championship in 1988, then totally dominated the series again in '89. He became almost cruelly efficient, able to win on any track, and judging his races so perfectly that, despite very strong opposition from the other factory Honda men, as well as the Yamaha riders, his victories quite often seemed inevitable.

MANUEL HERREROS

ALEX CRIVILLE

HAD he not been in the right place at the right time, he would probably never have given up working on a Valencia fruit farm, as his family has always done. Manuel was just a club racer when he got the chance to ride a bike being developed by one of Derbi's engineers in his spare time.

Born in 1963, he joined the Derbi team in 1985 as number two to Martinez. He remained as support rider, but when Martinez had so much trouble in the 1989 80 cc World Championship he became Derbi's title hope, clinching the last-ever 80 cc World Championship at the Czechoslovak Grand Prix.

WHEN he clinched the 1989 125 cc World Championship by winning the Czechoslovak Grand Prix, Alex became the youngest-ever World Champion. He was nineteen – and ten days younger than Johnny Cecotto was when he won the 350 cc title in 1975.

Born in 1970 in Barcelona, Criville started racing in 1985. He shot to prominence in the Spanish Grand Prix at Járama in 1987, riding a factory Derbi, when he finished second behind Jorge Martinez. He then left the Derbi team because he did not fit in with their team orders – and beat them in 1989 on his Cobas. Determined and professional, he never seems to get excited by his own success.

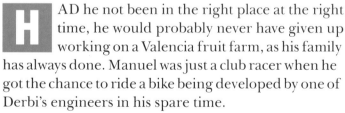

World Champion: 80 cc 1989

World Champion: 125 cc 1989

I T is not difficult to see how Webster and Hewitt won three straight Sidecar World Championships, in 1987, '88 and '89. With the ability to ride any sort of race that the circumstances demanded – a no-holds-barred, flat-out attack, a restrained tactical contest or a damage-limitation exercise – they became very much the team to emulate in the late Eighties.

Off track their approach was just as well balanced and their outfit the most reliable of all; they were the only team to score in all rounds of their championship-winning seasons. By avoiding some of the experimentation that their great rivals Biland, Streuer and Michel have gone in for, and by concentrating on first-class preparation they have achieved just the right combination of speed and reliability.

Father Mick Webster has been an important part of the team throughout his son's career and shares the mechanical work. He was a very successful sidecar grass track rider himself, three times a British champion, which no doubt helped him contribute to Steve's success.

The team achieved a high degree of professionalism on a limited budget and yet retained an open friendliness which has been appreciated by competitors, enthusiasts and the media. Steve concentrates full time on racing and organising the team, while Tony has tried to keep up his career as a civil engineer between racing commitments.

Born in 1960, Steve came to prominence by winning the British clubman's championship in 1982. The next season he was third in the British championship and scored his first World Championship points in his first international season. In successive seasons he progressed up the World Championship chart, and also won the British championship in 1985 and '86 before Grand Prix commitments made it impracticable to compete.

Three times sidecar champion Steve Webster *(right)* with passenger Tony Hewitt.

Randy Mamola: the best rider not to win a 500 cc
World Championship in the Eighties, he made himself
as popular for being a 'Clown Prince' as for being
incredibly fast.

Graeme Crosby: one of the sport's great naturals.
There is no doubt that this popular Kiwi retired too
soon, dispirited by the attitude of Giacomo Agostini,
for whom he rode in 1982 when he finished second in
the World Championship.

Jack Middelburg: tough little Dutchman who featured prominently in the 500 cc class in the early Eighties, winning the 1980 Dutch TT on a Yamaha and the 1981 British Grand Prix on a Suzuki. Lost his life in a racing accident in April 1984.

Raymond Roche: showed so much promise in 1984, when he finished third in the 500 cc World Championship on his Honda, that he was signed to ride as number two in the Marlboro Yamaha Agostini team. Roche was just one of the list who could not succeed in that position.

Niall Mackenzie: in an age when 500s had less power and corner speed was all-important, the Scot would have gone straight to the top. In the late Eighties he might have had more immediate success by staying in the 250 cc class.

Kevin Magee: a surprise recruit to the Kenny Roberts Lucky Strike Yamaha team for 1988, the Australian responded brilliantly to win the 500 cc Spanish Grand Prix that year. Always in the frame, he finished fifth in both the 1988 and 1989 World Championships before switching to Suzuki to team with Kevin Schwantz for 1990.

Rob McElnea: with so much natural ability there was no logical reason why he could not be a Grand Prix winner or even World Champion. Somewhere during his time as number two to Lawson in the Marlboro Yamaha team, though, things went wrong.

Jean-François Baldé: 200 Grands Prix is an impressive record by any standard. The Frenchman was second in the 250 cc World Championship in 1981 – and lesser men have been first.

Alain Michel: quiet, refined and approachable in the paddock but a demon on the track, the Frenchman was robbed of the Sidecar World Championship in 1986 when his helmet became unclipped in the final round.

Didier de Radiguès: from racing round the back streets of Brussels as a kid, he became a first-class Grand Prix competitor who missed out on the chance of winning the 350 cc World Championship in 1982 when water soaked his ignition in the final round and Toni Mang took the title.

Martin Wimmer: occasionally accused of being too intelligent to be a World Champion, he has always been one of the most professional competitors and a great man for machine experimentation.

Reinhold Roth: getting faster as he got older, and enjoying life more and more produced great results for the German who was second in the 250 cc World Championship in both 1987 and '89. No one could begrudge him his success.

Manfred Herweh: the likeable German worked his way to the top the hard way, tuning his own machinery. He finished second in the 250 cc World Championship in 1984 on his Rotax-engined Real.

Kevin Schwantz: no one has been more dramatic on
a 500. Incredibly skilled, Schwantz proved from early
in his Grand Prix career that he could make
the Suzuki dance.

Ron Haslam: a very fast gentleman racer who justifiably gained the reputation of being the best development rider in the 500 cc class. Ron's years with the Elf project helped that but did not help him win a Grand Prix.

Wayne Rainey: in trying to win the 1989 World
Championship, the Californian put together a season
that Eddie Lawson would have been proud of. Rainey
could not have known that Lawson was capable of
raising his game to the point where all Wayne's efforts
would only result in second place.

CRITICS' TOP TEN

JOHN BROWN

PETER CLIFFORD

DENIS JENKINSON

MICK WOOLLETT

1. Mike Hailwood
2. Geoff Duke
3. Eddie Lawson
4. Eric Oliver
5. Bob McIntyre
6. Kenny Roberts
7. John Surtees
8. Phil Read
9. Fergus Anderson
10. Jack Findlay

WHILE all my Top Ten are men who won races, and most of them were true World Champions in their class, winning was not my main criterion for choosing them. Much more important was how they won their races or their championships; it was the way they dominated the scene in their particular time, so that in their particular sphere they were the men who set the standards. Not just the standard of race winning, but the standards of riding, race tactics, track craft, style, their feeling for the sport and awareness that they were part of the overall sport of motor cycle racing, not only in their time but in the years that had gone before and the years to come.

There are some riders who would like you to think that they invented or discovered the sport and profession of motor cycle racing, totally ignoring everything that has gone before, and oblivious to what is to come. Rest assured that none of my Top Ten fall into that category.

This book surveys only 40 years of motor cycle racing; there were nearly 50 years of racing before this period, all of them important in creating and building the solid foundations of the sport on which we rest today. My Top Ten riders from the past 40 years all had the right outlook on being at the top of their profession, and conducted themselves in accordance with long-proven standards both on and off the track. They were all admirable ambassadors for our sport in every respect, and they were all professionals at the business of motor cycle racing in its highest form.

Above everything they all come under the heading of 'hard racers'. None of them had the need for an incentive to win – they were born winners – and whether first or last they rode with that aggressive will-to-win at all times. They all enjoyed victory and they could all accept defeat; it was part of being a truly professional motor cycle racer.

1. **Mike Hailwood**
2. **Phil Read**
3. **Eddie Lawson**
4. **Giacomo Agostini**
5. **Geoff Duke**
6. **John Surtees**
7. **Kenny Roberts**
8. **Barry Sheene**
9. **Jim Redman**
10. **Freddie Spencer**

YOU won't agree with my selection. It would be a miracle if you did! We all have our own ideas of who the top riders are – coloured by races we've seen, riders we've met and the machines they raced.

For me, Mike Hailwood was the greatest. He could ride anything and get the absolute best out of it – from 125 cc to 500 cc and above. He won World Championships in three classes and did it seemingly without effort – and certainly without any histrionics.

He proved that his skill and courage were enduring assets when he came out of retirement at the age of 38 to win the 1978 Formula One Isle of Man TT on a 860 cc Ducati with a record lap of 110.62 mph. And to show that he could master the modern two-stroke he returned in 1979 to win the 500 cc Senior TT on a works Suzuki, putting yet another lap record (114.02 mph) in the bag.

In my opinion Phil Read runs him close. Like Mike, Phil could ride anything. In fact, of the top class riders, he raced more different works machines than any other man – and he won World Championships in three classes, a feat achieved only by him and Hailwood. Read was a schemer – a master tactician who plotted his moves both on and off the track – and a very difficult man to beat.

By switching from Yamaha to Honda to win his fourth title Eddie Lawson has proved himself the best of the present-day riders and deserves to rank third above that charming Italian Giacomo Agostini, winner of a record 15 championships. True, a great many of Ago's wins were virtual walkovers because, in the early years of his career, the factory MV Agustas had no real rivals. But when the chips were down and Honda moved up into the 350 cc and 500 cc classes Ago showed his real worth, before switching to Yamaha to win his final 350 cc and 500 cc titles.

Geoff Duke just shades John Surtees because he won his titles when competition was fiercest – first on the works Nortons and then on the Gilera.

Kenny Roberts won three 500 cc titles to Sheene's two and he also got the better of Barry. And I place Jim Redman ninth, the only man in my top ten not to have won the 500 cc crown. Jim was the complete professional who went about the business of winning in a calm, almost detached way.

Tenth place goes to racing's great enigma – Freddie Spencer. Like Hailwood he was immensely talented and virtually unbeatable on his day. But, unlike Mike, his talent did not stand the test of time. It faded after a relatively brief span.

You'll notice that I do not rate any of the lightweight aces among those chosen. This is because all of the riders named could have moved down a class or two and still won, but there are very few who could have moved up – in other words, the 500 cc division is the one that really sorts the men from the boys.

1. Eddie Lawson
2. Phil Read
3. Jarno Saarinen
4. Mike Hailwood
5. Giacomo Agostini
6. Kenny Roberts
7. Geoff Duke
8. Barry Sheene
9. Angel Nieto
10. Freddie Spencer

CALIFORNIAN Eddie Lawson achieved what no other rider had succeeded in doing in the 41 years of post-war Grand Prix racing when he retained the 500 cc World Championship for two consecutive years while riding different makes of machine.

After giving Marlboro Yamaha the major title three times between 1984 and 1988, Lawson dramatically moved across to Rothmans Honda in 1989 and, against the odds, again came out on top. In the early stages of the campaign his chances of making the breakthrough looked slim as he lost ground to fellow-Californian Wayne Rainey, and as he battled to get on terms with the Honda that was different in nearly every respect to the Yamaha he had grown up with in Grand Prix racing.

But then the professionalism and skill that, for me, makes Eddie Lawson the greatest World Champion so far, shone through. He levelled, and one of the pretenders to the crown had to crack. In Sweden, with only two more rounds to go, Rainey crashed and Lawson was in front for the first time – and heading for that championship again.

I go for Phil Read in second place not for his works Yamaha days in the Sixties, when he won four championships, but for his brave efforts as a privateer in 1971 which were rewarded with the 250 cc title. He organised his team well to take on Yamaha-supported rivals and despite painful injuries dragged himself up to Finland in search of points that turned out to be decisive at the final count.

Finn Jarno Saarinen had all the makings of a super champion before he was tragically killed during the 1973 Italian Grand Prix at Monza. The 250 cc title in 1972 is the only one that bears his name in the record books, but he certainly would have added many more.

Arguably the greatest all-rounder in road racing, Mike Hailwood is my choice for fourth place, and fifteen times World Champion Giacomo Agostini also has to be among the greats. He ensured this not during his all-conquering days with MV in the late Sixties and early Seventies, but when he switched from four-stroke to two-stroke and won the 1975 500 cc World Championship, beating arch-rival Read who had taken his MV ride.

Then there's Kenny Roberts, who dominated when he made it three 500s in a row; Geoff Duke, the first rider to clinch a double in the 350 and 500 cc classes in 1951; Barry Sheene, not only a double champion but also the rider who did so much for the sport worldwide; and Angel Nieto, the small class wizard for well over a decade, whose number of championship wins is second only to Agostini.

Last but not least comes Freddie Spencer, who ended his career on a bitterly disappointing note after showing the greatest potential in recent years when he became the only rider ever to win the 250 cc and 500 cc championships in the same year – and at a time when riders in both classes cringed at the suggestion of mixing the two.

My reserve, Kork Ballington, looked so impressive when he took Kawasaki to 250/350 doubles in 1978 and 1979 that he really warrants a place too.

PETER CLIFFORD'S TOP TEN

1.	**Mike Hailwood**
2.	**Kenny Roberts**
3.	**Angel Nieto**
4.	**Giacomo Agostini**
5.	**Geoff Duke**
6.	**Phil Read**
7.	**John Surtees**
8.	**Carlo Ubbiali**
9.	**Eddie Lawson**
10.	**Jim Redman**

APART from the fact that Mike Hailwood is my all-time number one, and there was never any doubt about his rightful place, the rest of the table demanded an impossible choice. In the end the second position was given to Kenny Roberts, because of my feeling that, like Hailwood, he would have won on any sort of machine under any circumstances in any era.

The remainder of the Top Ten qualified by dint of that combination of natural talent, technical application and tactical understanding that makes champions – and some also had the guile to make sure that they were on the right machines at the right time.

Against those who argue that there were men like Nieto and Agostini who won World Championships either on superior machinery or against lesser riders, I would counter that, in other years, they also beat some of the best riders in the world on equal equipment.

There are so many names that I wish could have been included, like Bill Ivy, Jarno Saarinen and Bob McIntyre – men who lacked nothing in ability but did lack the good fortune to demonstrate their talent for long enough on the right equipment.

Then, reappraising the pros and cons again, one could so easily reorder the Top Ten, or swap in such names as Toni Mang, Freddie Spencer and Kork Ballington.

I found it totally impossible to consider the sidecar competitors alongside the solo men, and hence there is no mention of Oliver, Deubel, Enders, Streuer, Biland or Webster.

In one respect, the whole balance demanded of a champion has changed in the timespan covered by this book. The effects of greater circuit safety and track quality, superior tyre and engine performance as well as the depth of competition and its rewards are almost incomparable from one decade to the next. But then, when you see a new star, such as Kevin Schwantz, there can be no doubt that he would have succeeded in any decade. He could surely have lapped the TT course at over 100 mph on a Manx Norton, won at the old Nürburgring or at Spa in the rain, and raced even pre-war machines with no suspension. But, to be certain of such things, you have to see them with your own eyes. Record books cannot help.

1949
125 cc NELLO PAGANI (Mondial)
250 cc BRUNO RUFFO (Moto Guzzi)
350 cc FREDDIE FRITH (Velocette)
500 cc LES GRAHAM (AJS)
Sidecar ERIC OLIVER/
      DENIS JENKINSON (Norton)

1950
125 cc BRUNO RUFFO (Mondial)
250 cc DARIO AMBROSINI (Benelli)
350 cc BOB FOSTER (Velocette)
500 cc UMBERTO MASETTI (Gilera)
Sidecar ERIC OLIVER/
      LORENZO DOBELLI (Norton)

1951
125 cc CARLO UBBIALI (Mondial)
250 cc BRUNO RUFFO (Moto Guzzi)
350 cc GEOFF DUKE (Norton)
500 cc GEOFF DUKE (Norton)
Sidecar ERIC OLIVER/
      LORENZO DOBELLI (Norton)

1952
125 cc CECIL SANDFORD (MV Agusta)
250 cc ENRICO LORENZETTI (Moto Guzzi)
350 cc GEOFF DUKE (Norton)
500 cc UMBERTO MASETTI (Gilera)
Sidecar CYRIL SMITH/BOB CLEMENTS (Norton)

1953
125 cc WERNER HAAS (NSU)
250 cc WERNER HAAS (NSU)
350 cc FERGUS ANDERSON (Moto Guzzi)
500 cc GEOFF DUKE (Gilera)
Sidecar ERIC OLIVER/STAN DIBBEN (Norton)

1954
125 cc RUPERT HOLLAUS (NSU)
250 cc WERNER HAAS (NSU)
350 cc FERGUS ANDERSON (Moto Guzzi)
500 cc GEOFF DUKE (Gilera)
Sidecar WILLI NOLL/FRITZ CRON (BMW)

1955
125 cc CARLO UBBIALI (MV Agusta)
250 cc HERMANN-PETER MULLER (NSU)
350 cc BILL LOMAS (Moto Guzzi)
500 cc GEOFF DUKE (Gilera)
Sidecar WILLI FAUST/KARL REMMERT (BMW)

1956
125 cc CARLO UBBIALI (MV Agusta)
250 cc CARLO UBBIALI (MV Agusta)
350 cc BILL LOMAS (Moto Guzzi)
500 cc JOHN SURTEES (MV Agusta)
Sidecar WILLI NOLL/FRITZ CRON (BMW)

1957
125 cc TARQUINIO PROVINI (Mondial)
250 cc CECIL SANDFORD (Mondial)
350 cc KEITH CAMPBELL (Moto Guzzi)
500 cc LIBERO LIBERATI (Gilera)
Sidecar FRITZ HILLEBRAND/
      MANFRED GRUNWALD (BMW)

1958
125 cc CARLO UBBIALI (MV Agusta)
250 cc TARQUINIO PROVINI (MV Agusta)
350 cc JOHN SURTEES (MV Agusta)
500 cc JOHN SURTEES (MV Agusta)
Sidecar WALTER SCHNEIDER/
      HANS STRAUSS (BMW)

1959
125 cc CARLO UBBIALI (MV Agusta)
250 cc CARLO UBBIALI (MV Agusta)
350 cc JOHN SURTEES (MV Agusta)
500 cc JOHN SURTEES (MV Agusta)
Sidecar WALTER SCHNEIDER/
      HANS STRAUSS (BMW)

1960
125 cc CARLO UBBIALI (MV Agusta)
250 cc CARLO UBBIALI (MV Agusta)
350 cc JOHN SURTEES (MV Agusta)
500 cc JOHN SURTEES (MV Agusta)
Sidecar HELMUT FATH/
      ALFRED WOHLGEMUTH (BMW)

1961
125 cc TOM PHILLIS (Honda)
250 cc MIKE HAILWOOD (Honda)
350 cc GARY HOCKING (MV Agusta)
500 cc GARY HOCKING (MV Agusta)
Sidecar MAX DEUBEL/EMIL HORNER (BMW)

1962
50 cc ERNST DEGNER (Suzuki)
125 cc LUIGI TAVERI (Honda)
250 cc JIM REDMAN (Honda)
350 cc JIM REDMAN (Honda)
500 cc MIKE HAILWOOD (MV Agusta)
Sidecar MAX DEUBEL/EMIL HORNER (BMW)

1963
50 cc HUGH ANDERSON (Suzuki)
125 cc HUGH ANDERSON (Suzuki)
250 cc JIM REDMAN (Honda)
350 cc JIM REDMAN (Honda)
500 cc MIKE HAILWOOD (MV Agusta)
Sidecar MAX DEUBEL/EMIL HORNER (BMW)

1964
50 cc HUGH ANDERSON (Suzuki)
125 cc LUIGI TAVERI (Honda)
250 cc PHIL READ (Yamaha)
350 cc JIM REDMAN (Honda)
500 cc MIKE HAILWOOD (MV Agusta)
Sidecar MAX DEUBEL/EMIL HORNER (BMW)

1965
50 cc RALPH BRYANS (Honda)
125 cc HUGH ANDERSON (Suzuki)
250 cc PHIL READ (Yamaha)
350 cc JIM REDMAN (Honda)
500 cc MIKE HAILWOOD (MV Agusta)
Sidecar FRITZ SCHEIDEGGER/
     JOHN ROBINSON (BMW)

1966
50 cc HANS-GEORG ANSCHEIDT (Suzuki)
125 cc LUIGI TAVERI (Honda)
250 cc MIKE HAILWOOD (Honda)
350 cc MIKE HAILWOOD (Honda)
500 cc GIACOMO AGOSTINI (MV Agusta)
Sidecar FRITZ SCHEIDEGGER/
     JOHN ROBINSON (BMW)

1967
50 cc HANS-GEORG ANSCHEIDT (Suzuki)
125 cc BILL IVY (Yamaha)
250 cc MIKE HAILWOOD (Honda)
350 cc MIKE HAILWOOD (Honda)
500 cc GIACOMO AGOSTINI (MV Agusta)
Sidecar KLAUS ENDERS/
     RALF ENGELHARDT (BMW)

1968
50 cc HANS-GEORG ANSCHEIDT (Suzuki)
125 cc PHIL READ (Yamaha)
250 cc PHIL READ (Yamaha)
350 cc GIACOMO AGOSTINI (MV Agusta)
500 cc GIACOMO AGOSTINI (MV Agusta)
Sidecar HELMUT FATH/
     WOLFGANG KALAUCH (URS)

1969
50 cc ANGEL NIETO (Derbi)
125 cc DAVE SIMMONDS (Kawasaki)
250 cc KEL CARRUTHERS (Benelli)
350 cc GIACOMO AGOSTINI (MV Agusta)
500 cc GIACOMO AGOSTINI (MV Agusta)
Sidecar KLAUS ENDERS/
     RALF ENGELHARDT (BMW)

1970

50 cc ANGEL NIETO (Derbi)
125 cc DIETER BRAUN (Suzuki)
250 cc ROD GOULD (Yamaha)
350 cc GIACOMO AGOSTINI (MV Agusta)
500 cc GIACOMO AGOSTINI (MV Agusta)
Sidecar KLAUS ENDERS/
      WOLFGANG KALAUCH (BMW)

1971

50 cc JAN DE VRIES (Kreidler)
125 cc ANGEL NIETO (Derbi)
250 cc PHIL READ (Yamaha)
350 cc GIACOMO AGOSTINI (MV Agusta)
500 cc GIACOMO AGOSTINI (MV Agusta)
Sidecar HORST OWESLE/
      PETER RUTTERFORD (URS)

1972

50 cc ANGEL NIETO (Derbi)
125 cc ANGEL NIETO (Derbi)
250 cc JARNO SAARINEN (Yamaha)
350 cc GIACOMO AGOSTINI (MV Agusta)
500 cc GIACOMO AGOSTINI (MV Agusta)
Sidecar KLAUS ENDERS/
      RALF ENGELHARDT (BMW)

1973

50 cc JAN DE VRIES (Kreidler)
125 cc KENT ANDERSSON (Yamaha)
250 cc DIETER BRAUN (Yamaha)
350 cc GIACOMO AGOSTINI (MV Agusta)
500 cc PHIL READ (MV Agusta)
Sidecar KLAUS ENDERS/
      RALF ENGELHARDT (BMW)

1974

50 cc HENK VAN KESSEL (Kreidler)
125 cc KENT ANDERSSON (Yamaha)
250 cc WALTER VILLA (Harley-Davidson)
350 cc GIACOMO AGOSTINI (Yamaha)
500 cc PHIL READ (MV Agusta)
Sidecar KLAUS ENDERS/
      RALF ENGELHARDT (BMW)

1975

50 cc ANGEL NIETO (Kreidler)
125 cc PAOLO PILERI (Morbidelli)
250 cc WALTER VILLA (Harley-Davidson)
350 cc JOHNNY CECOTTO (Yamaha)
500 cc GIACOMO AGOSTINI (Yamaha)
Sidecar ROLF STEINHAUSEN/
      SEPP HUBER (Konig)

1976

50 cc ANGEL NIETO (Bultaco)
125 cc PIER-PAOLO BIANCHI (Morbidelli)
250 cc WALTER VILLA (Harley-Davidson)
350 cc WALTER VILLA (Harley-Davidson)
500 cc BARRY SHEENE (Suzuki)
Sidecar ROLF STEINHAUSEN/
      SEPP HUBER (Konig)

1977

50 cc ANGEL NIETO (Bultaco)
125 cc PIER-PAOLO BIANCHI (Morbidelli)
250 cc MARIO LEGA (Morbidelli)
350 cc TAKAZUMI KATAYAMA (Yamaha)
500 cc BARRY SHEENE (Suzuki)
Sidecar GEORGE O'DELL/KENNY ARTHUR
      and CLIFF HOLLAND (Seymaz-Yamaha)

1978

50 cc RICARDO TORMO (Bultaco)
125 cc EUGENIO LAZZARINI (MBA)
250 cc KORK BALLINGTON (Kawasaki)
350 cc KORK BALLINGTON (Kawasaki)
500 cc KENNY ROBERTS (Yamaha)
Sidecar ROLF BILAND/
      KENNY WILLIAMS (Beo/TTM Yamaha)

1979

50 cc EUGENIO LAZZARINI (Kreidler)
125 cc ANGEL NIETO (Minarelli)
250 cc KORK BALLINGTON (Kawasaki)
350 cc KORK BALLINGTON (Kawasaki)
500 cc KENNY ROBERTS (Yamaha)
Sidecar ROLF BILAND/
      KURT WALTISPERG (TTM Yamaha)

1980
50 cc EUGENIO LAZZARINI (Kreidler)
125 cc PIER-PAOLO BIANCHI (MBA)
250 cc ANTON MANG (Kawasaki)
350 cc JON EKEROLD (Yamaha)
500 cc KENNY ROBERTS (Yamaha)
Sidecar JOCK TAYLOR/
      BENGA JOHANSSON (Yamaha)

1981
50 cc RICARDO TORMO (Bultaco)
125 cc ANGEL NIETO (Minarelli)
250 cc ANTON MANG (Kawasaki)
350 cc ANTON MANG (Kawasaki)
500 cc MARCO LUCCHINELLI (Suzuki)
Sidecar ROLF BILAND/
      KURT WALTISPERG (LCR-Yamaha)

1982
50 cc STEFAN DÖRFLINGER (Kreidler)
125 cc ANGEL NIETO (Garelli)
250 cc JEAN-LOUIS TOURNADRE (Yamaha)
350 cc ANTON MANG (Kawasaki)
500 cc FRANCO UNCINI (Suzuki)
Sidecar WERNER SCHWÄRZEL/
      ANDREAS HUBER (Seymaz-Yamaha)

1983
50 cc STEFAN DÖRFLINGER (Kreidler)
125 cc ANGEL NIETO (Garelli)
250 cc CARLOS LAVADO (Yamaha)
500 cc FREDDIE SPENCER (Honda)
Sidecar ROLF BILAND/
      KURT WALTISPERG (LCR-Yamaha)

1984
80 cc STEFAN DÖRFLINGER (Zundapp)
125 cc ANGEL NIETO (Garelli)
250 cc CHRISTIAN SARRON (Yamaha)
500 cc EDDIE LAWSON (Yamaha)
Sidecar EGBERT STREUER/
      BERNIE SCHNIEDERS (LCR-Yamaha)

1985
80 cc STEFAN DÖRFLINGER (Krauser)
125 cc FAUSTO GRESINI (Garelli)
250 cc FREDDIE SPENCER (Honda)
500 cc FREDDIE SPENCER (Honda)
Sidecar EGBERT STREUER/
      BERNIE SCHNIEDERS (LCR-Yamaha)

1986
80 cc JORGE MARTINEZ (Derbi)
125 cc LUCA CADALORA (Garelli)
250 cc CARLOS LAVADO (Yamaha)
500 cc EDDIE LAWSON (Yamaha)
Sidecar EGBERT STREUER/
      BERNIE SCHNIEDERS (LCR-Yamaha)

1987
80 cc JORGE MARTINEZ (Derbi)
125 cc FAUSTO GRESINI (Garelli)
250 cc ANTON MANG (Honda)
500 cc WAYNE GARDNER (Honda)
Sidecar STEVE WEBSTER/
      TONY HEWITT (LCR-Yamaha)

1988
80 cc JORGE MARTINEZ (Derbi)
125 cc JORGE MARTINEZ (Derbi)
250 cc SITO PONS (Honda)
500 cc EDDIE LAWSON (Yamaha)
Sidecar STEVE WEBSTER/
      TONY HEWITT (LCR-Yamaha)

1989
80 cc MANUEL HERREROS (Derbi)
125 cc ALEX CRIVILLE (Cobas)
250 cc SITO PONS (Honda)
500 cc EDDIE LAWSON (Honda)
Sidecar STEVE WEBSTER/
      TONY HEWITT (LCR-Yamaha)

Note: the 350 cc class was dropped after the 1982 season.
The 50 cc class was replaced by the 80 cc in 1984.

	50/80 cc	125 cc	250 cc	350 cc	500 cc	Sidecar	Total
GIACOMO AGOSTINI, Italy				7	8		15
ANGEL NIETO, Spain	6	7					13
MIKE HAILWOOD, GB			3	2	4		9
CARLO UBBIALI, Italy		6	3				9
PHIL READ, GB		1	4		2		7
JOHN SURTEES, GB				3	4		7
GEOFF DUKE, GB				2	4		6
KLAUS ENDERS, West Germany						6	6
JIM REDMAN, Rhodesia			2	4			6
ANTON MANG, West Germany			3	2			5
HUGH ANDERSON, New Zealand	2	2					4
KORK BALLINGTON, South Africa			2	2			4
ROLF BILAND, Switzerland						4	4
MAX DEUBEL, West Germany						4	4
STEFAN DÖRFLINGER, Switzerland	4						4
EDDIE LAWSON, USA					4		4
JORGE MARTINEZ, Spain	3	1					4
ERIC OLIVER, GB						4	4
WALTER VILLA, Italy			3	1			4
HANS-GEORG ANSCHEIDT, West Germany	3						3
PIER-PAOLO BIANCHI, Italy		3					3
WERNER HAAS, West Germany		1	2				3
EUGENIO LAZZARINI, Italy	2	1					3
KENNY ROBERTS, USA					3		3
BRUNO RUFFO, Italy		1	2				3
FREDDIE SPENCER, USA			1		2		3
EGBERT STREUER, Holland						3	3
LUIGI TAVERI, Switzerland		3					3
STEVE WEBSTER, GB						3	3
FERGUS ANDERSON, GB				2			2
KENT ANDERSSON, Sweden		2					2
DIETER BRAUN, West Germany		1	1				2
HELMUT FATH, West Germany						2	2
FAUSTO GRESINI, Italy		2					2
GARY HOCKING, Rhodesia				1	1		2
CARLOS LAVADO, Venezuela			2				2
BILL LOMAS, GB				2			2
UMBERTO MASETTI, Italy					2		2
WILLI NOLL, West Germany						2	2
SITO PONS, Spain			2				2
TARQUINIO PROVINI, Italy		1	1				2
CECIL SANDFORD, GB		1	1				2
FRITZ SCHEIDEGGER, Switzerland						2	2
WALTER SCHNEIDER, West Germany						2	2

	50/80 cc	125 cc	250 cc	350 cc	500 cc	Sidecar	Total
BARRY SHEENE, GB					2		2
ROLF STEINHAUSEN, West Germany						2	2
RICARDO TORMO, Spain	2						2
JAN DE VRIES, Holland	2						2
DARIO AMBROSINI, Italy			1				1
RALPH BRYANS, Ireland	1						1
LUCA CADALORA, Italy		1					1
KEITH CAMPBELL, Australia				1			1
KEL CARRUTHERS, Australia			1				1
JOHNNY CECOTTO, Venezuela				1			1
ALEX CRIVILLE, Spain		1					1
ERNST DEGNER, West Germany	1						1
JON EKEROLD, South Africa				1			1
WILLI FAUST, West Germany						1	1
BOB FOSTER, GB				1			1
FREDDIE FRITH, GB				1			1
WAYNE GARDNER, Australia					1		1
ROD GOULD, GB			1				1
LES GRAHAM, GB					1		1
MANUEL HERREROS, Spain	1						1
FRITZ HILLEBRAND, West Germany						1	1
RUPERT HOLLAUS, Austria		1					1
BILL IVY, GB		1					1
TAKAZUMI KATAYAMA, Japan				1			1
HENK VAN KESSEL, Holland	1						1
MARIO LEGA, Italy			1				1
LIBERO LIBERATI, Italy					1		1
ENRICO LORENZETTI, Italy			1				1
MARCO LUCCHINELLI, Italy					1		1
HERMANN-PETER MULLER, West Germany			1				1
GEORGE O'DELL, GB						1	1
HORST OWESLE, West Germany						1	1
NELLO PAGANI, Italy		1					1
TOM PHILLIS, Australia		1					1
PAOLO PILERI, Italy		1					1
JARNO SAARINEN, Finland			1				1
CHRISTIAN SARRON, France			1				1
WERNER SCHWÄRZEL, West Germany						1	1
DAVE SIMMONDS, GB		1					1
CYRIL SMITH, GB						1	1
JEAN-LOUIS TOURNADRE, France			1				1
JOCK TAYLOR, GB						1	1
FRANCO UNCINI, Italy					1		1

THE GRAND PRIX RIDERS

Colour Photographs:

ALLSPORT
Pages: 73, 74 *(below)*, 75

ALLSPORT/STEVE POWELL
Pages: 74 *(above)*, 76

MALCOLM BRYAN
Pages: 77-79, 80 *(bottom)*

NICK NICHOLLS
Pages: 68-69

MICK WOOLLETT
Pages: 65-67, 70-72, 80 *(top and middle)*

**Black and white photographs
have been contributed by:**
François Beau
Malcolm Bryan
Maurice Büla
Champion
Hazel Coad
Richard Francis
Jan Heese
Brian Kelly
Helmut Krackowizer
Nick Nicholls
Peter Preissler
Rothmans
Karl Schleuter
Mick Woollett